Oxford AQA GCSE History (9-1)

America 1920-1973

Opportunity and Inequality

Revision Guide

 RECAP    APPLY    REVIEW    SUCCEED

AUTHOR AND SERIES EDITOR
Aaron Wilkes

 OXFORD

OXFORD
UNIVERSITY PRESS

Great Clarendon Street, Oxford, OX2 6DP, United Kingdom

Oxford University Press is a department of the University of Oxford.

It furthers the University's objective of excellence in research, scholarship, and education by publishing worldwide. Oxford is a registered trade mark of Oxford University Press in the UK and in certain other countries.

British Library Cataloguing in Publication Data

Data available

978-0-19-843282-1

Digital edition 978-0-19-843283-8

3 5 7 9 10 8 6 4

Paper used in the production of this book is a natural, recyclable product made from wood grown in sustainable forests.

The manufacturing process conforms to the environmental regulations of the country of origin.

Printed in India by Multivista Global Pvt. Ltd

Acknowledgements

Cover: Bettmann/Getty Images

Artworks: QBS Learning

Photos: p20: GoodStudio/Shutterstock; **p21**: GoodStudio/Shutterstock

The publisher would like to thank Jon Cloake for his work on the Student Book on which this Revision Guide is based and David Rawlings for reviewing this Revision Guide.

We are grateful for permission to include extracts from copyright material:

Barbara Epstein: 'What happened to the women's movement', *Monthly Review*, Vol 53: 1 (May, 2001) used by permission of Monthly Review Foundation via Copyright Clearance Center

Lee Grant: interview for *Best Years 1946-1952*, episode 8 of the documentary series *The Century: America's Time*, copyright © ABC News 1999, used by permission of American Broadcasting Corporation (ABC News)

Jennifer Lee: from her film *Feminist: Stories from Women's Liberation* at www.feministstories.com, used by permission of Jennifer Lee

Frances Perkins: *The Roosevelt I Knew* (Penguin 2011) first published Viking New York 1946; used by permission of the author's grandson, Tom Coggeshall, and the Frances Perkins Center

Studs R Terkel: *The Studs Terkel Reader: My American Century* (The New Press, 2007), compilation copyright © 1997 by The New Press, text copyright © Studs Terkel, used by permission of The New Press, www.thenewpress.com

We have made every effort to trace and contact all copyright holders before publication. If notified of any errors or omissions, the publisher will be happy to rectify these at the earliest opportunity.

Links to third party websites are provided by Oxford in good faith and for information only. Oxford disclaims any responsibility for the materials contained in any third party website referenced in this work.

Contents

RECAP   **APPLY**   **REVIEW**

Part one:

American people and the 'Boom'

Part two:

Bust – Americans' experiences of the Depression and the New Deal

Contents

Part three:
Post-war America

Introduction

The *Oxford AQA GCSE History* textbook series has been developed by an expert team led by Jon Cloake and Aaron Wilkes. This matching revision guide offers you step-by-step strategies to master your AQA Period Study: America 1920–1973 Opportunity and Inequality exam skills, and the structured revision approach of **Recap, Apply and Review** to prepare you for exam success.

Use the **Progress checklists** on pages 3–4 to keep track of your revision, and use the traffic light feature on each page to monitor your confidence level on each topic. Other exam practice and revision features include **Top revision tips** on page 6, and the **'How to...'** guides for each exam question type on pages 7–9.

 RECAP Each chapter recaps key events and developments through easy-to-digest chunks and visual diagrams. **Key terms** appear in bold and red; they are defined in the glossary. 📖 indicates the relevant Oxford AQA History Student Book pages so you can easily reread the textbook for further revision.

SUMMARY highlights the most important facts at the end of each chapter.

TIMELINE ⏱ provides a short list of dates to help you remember key events.

 APPLY Each revision activity is designed to help drill your understanding of facts, and then progress towards applying your knowledge to exam questions.

These targeted revision activities are written specifically for this guide, which will help you apply your knowledge towards the four exam questions in your AQA America 1920–1973 Opportunity and Inequality exam paper:

INTERPRETATION ANALYSIS   **DESCRIBE**   **IN WHAT WAYS**   **BULLET POINTS**

 Examiner Tip highlights key parts of an exam question, and gives you hints on how to avoid common mistakes in exams.

 Revision Skills provides different revision techniques. Research shows that using a variety of revision styles can help cement your revision.

 Review gives you helpful reminders about how to check your answers and how to revise further.

 REVIEW Throughout each chapter, you can review and reflect on the work you have done, and find advice on how to further refresh your knowledge.

You can tick off the Review column from the Progress checklists as you work through this revision guide. **Activity answers guidance** and the **Exam practice** sections with full sample student answers also help you to review your own work.

Top revision tips

Getting your revision right

It is perfectly natural to feel anxious when exam time approaches. The best way to keep on top of the stress is to be organised!

3 months to go

Plan: create a realistic revision timetable, and stick to it!

Track your progress: use the Progress checklists (pages 3–4) to help you track your revision. It will help you stick to your revision plan.

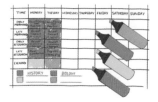

Be realistic: revise in regular, small chunks, of around 30 minutes. Reward yourself with 10 minute breaks – you will be amazed how much more you'll remember.

Positive thinking: motivate yourself by turning your negative thoughts to positive ones. Instead of asking *'why can't I remember this topic at all?'* ask yourself *'what different techniques can I try to improve my memory?'*

Organise: make sure you have everything you need – your revision books, coloured pens, index cards, sticky notes, paper, etc. Find a quiet place where you are comfortable. Divide your notes into sections that are easy to use.

Timeline: create a timeline with colour-coded sticky notes, to make sure you remember important dates relating to the three parts of the America Period Study (use the Timeline on page 11 as a starting point).

Practise: ask your teachers for practice questions or past papers.

Revision techniques

Using a variety of revision techniques can help you remember information, so try out different methods:

- Make **flashcards**, using both sides of the card to test yourself on key figures, dates and definitions
- **Colour-code** your notebooks
- **Reread** your textbook or copy out your notes
- Create **mind-maps** for complicated topics
- Draw **pictures** and symbols that spring to mind
- Group study
- Find a **buddy** or group to revise with and test you
- Listen to revision **podcasts** or watch revision **clips**
- Work through the **revision activities** in this guide

Revision tips to help you pass your America 1920–1973 Opportunity and Inequality exam

1 month to go

Key concepts: make sure you understand key concepts for this topic, such as democracy, inequality, communism, poverty, discrimination and prejudice. If you're unsure, attend revision sessions and ask your teacher.

Identify your weaknesses: which topics or question types are easier and which are more challenging for you? Schedule more time to revise the challenging topics or question types.

Make it stick: find memorable ways to remember chronology, using fun rhymes, or doodles, for example.

Take a break: do something completely different during breaks – listen to music, take a short walk, make a cup of tea, for example.

Check your answers: answer the exam questions in this guide, *then* check the Activity answers guidance at the end of the guide to practise applying your knowledge to exam questions.

Understand your mark scheme: review the Mark scheme (page 10) for each exam question, and make sure you understand how you will be marked.

Master your exam skills: study and remember the How to master your exam skills steps (pages 7–9) for each AQA question type – it will help you plan your answers quickly!

Time yourself: practise making plans and answering exam questions within the recommended time limits.

Take mock exams seriously: you can learn from them how to manage your time better under exam conditions.

Rest well: make sure your phone and laptop are put away at least an hour before bed. This will help you rest better.

On the big day

Sleep early: don't work through the night, get a good night's sleep.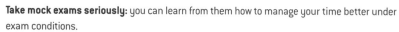

Be prepared: make sure you know where and when the exam is, and leave plenty of time to get there.

Check: make sure you have all your equipment in advance, including spare pens!

Drink and eat healthily: avoid too much caffeine or junk food. Water is best – if you are 5% dehydrated, then your concentration drops 20%.

Stay focused: don't listen to people who might try to wind you up about what might come up in the exam – they don't know any more than you.

Good luck!

Master your exam skills

Get to grips with your Paper 1: America 1920–1973 Opportunity and Inequality

The Paper 1 exam lasts 1 hour 45 minutes, and you have to answer ten questions covering two topics. The first six questions (worth 40 marks) will cover your America topic; the last four questions (40 marks) will cover your Conflict and Tension topic. Here, you will find details about what to expect from the first six questions which relate to America, and advice on how to master your exam skills.

You should spend about 50 minutes in total on the America questions – see pages 8–9 for how long to spend on each question. **The six questions will always follow this pattern:**

▼ **INTERPRETATION A**

▼ **INTERPRETATION B**

01 How does **Interpretation B** differ from **Interpretation A** about…? Explain your answer using **Interpretations A** and **B**. | 4 marks |

02 Why might the authors of **Interpretations A** and **B** have a different interpretation about …? Explain your answer using **Interpretations A** and **B** and your contextual knowledge. | 4 marks |

03 Which interpretation do you find more convincing about …? Explain your answers using **Interpretations A** and **B** and your contextual knowledge. | 8 marks |

04 Describe two… | 4 marks |

05 In what ways…? Explain your answer. | 8 marks |

06 Which of the following was the more important reason…

☐ _____

☐ _____?

Explain your answer with reference to both bullet points. | 12 marks |

REVISION SKILLS

Read the *Wider World Depth Study Revision Guide* for help on the last four questions of Paper 1.

EXAMINER TIP

The **caption** for the interpretations is key. It gives you the provenance, which are the details about when or where it was written or said, and the author's background.

EXAMINER TIP

The actual **content** of the interpretations is important for Questions 1 and 3. You will only discuss the provenance in answer to Question 2.

EXAMINER TIP

Question 6 will always have two bullet points referring to factors or events. You need to show you can evaluate by deciding which of the bullet points to argue for. This question is worth 12 marks, so make sure you give yourself enough time to plan and write your essay.

REVIEW

If you find interpretations challenging, look out for the **INTERPRETATION ANALYSIS** activities throughout this guide to help you revise and drill your understanding of the interpretation questions. Look out for the **REVISION SKILLS** ✓ tips too, to inspire you to find the revision strategies that work for you!

How to master the 'interpretation' questions

Here are the steps to consider when answering the three interpretation questions. Remember that each question targets a different aspect of the interpretations.

Question 1

- **Content:** Read the question and the two interpretations carefully, and analyse the contents of both interpretations. What is different in the interpretations? Where does the content differ? Write at least 2–3 differences down. Make sure you refer to both **Interpretations A** and **B**.

- ⏱ Spend about 5 minutes answering this 4-mark question.

Question 2

- **Context:** This question is about the circumstances in which the interpretations were said/written. What situation was the person in that made them say what they said? Make sure you use the captions (provenances) of each interpretation to help you answer this question.

- ⏱ Spend about 5 minutes on this 4-mark question.

Question 3

- **Comment:** First, what historical facts can you use to support or challenge each author's view? Use the knowledge you have based on what you've studied about this topic. Again, make sure you comment on both interpretations in turn.

- **Conclude:** Finally, comment on which you find most convincing – which interpretation fits better with what you know about the history of this topic? Your conclusion on which is most convincing should be based on the history that happened, not on who the author is.

- ⏱ Spend about 10 minutes on this 8-mark question.

How to master the 'describe' question

Here are the steps to consider when answering the 'describe' question.

Question 4

- **Two features:** You have to show what you know and understand about two key features or issues of this period. Make sure you name the two features, then write some historical facts about each of those features.

- ⏱ Spend about 5 minutes on this 4-mark question.

How to master the 'in what ways' question

Here are the steps to consider when answering the 'in what ways' question.

Question 5

- **What changed and what caused the changes:** You have to explain how a particular group of people experienced changes due to events or government decisions. What were the causes of the changes, and what were the results? Name 2–3 changes, causes, or consequences, then write some facts about each change/cause/consequence.

- ⏱ Spend about 10 minutes on this 8-mark question.

How to master the 'bullet points' question

The last question on America in Paper 1 will always relate to two bullet points. You have to compare the two things named in the bullet points, and come up with a judgement (conclusion) about which is more important. Here are the steps to consider:

Question 6

- **Read the question carefully:** What topic is the question asking about? The topic is located before the colon. Underline the topic and the dates to help you focus your answer.

- **Plan your essay:** Ask yourself, 'what are the historical facts or concepts I know about how each bullet point affected the topic?' Spend 1–2 minutes drawing a quick mind-map to establish your main arguments/historical evidence on each of the bullet points. Try to structure your essay answer in four paragraphs, starting with an introduction, two main paragraphs, and a conclusion.

- **Introduce your argument:** Make sure you name the key topic and dates, and the two bullet points.

- **Analyse each bullet:** For each bullet point, write at least one paragraph about why that point may be more important, or what the impact of the bullet point was.

- **Conclude your argument:** It is important to come to a conclusion. Decide (judge) which bullet point you think was more important, and summarise your argument.

- ⏱ Spend about 15 minutes on this 12-mark question.

> **REVIEW**
>
> You can find sample student answers to each question type in the **Exam practice** pages at the end of this guide.

EXAMINER TIP

Don't forget you will have to answer four more questions relating to your Conflict and Tension topic in Paper 1. Ensure you leave enough time to complete both sections of Paper 1! You are advised to spend 50 minutes on your Conflict and Tension topic in the exam.

AQA GCSE History mark schemes

Below are simplified versions of the AQA mark schemes, to help you understand the marking criteria for your **Paper 1: America** exam.

Level	Interpretation question 1
2	• Developed analysis of the two interpretations. • Differences are explained with relevant facts. 3–4 marks
1	• Simple analysis of one or two interpretations. • Differences are named. 1–2 marks

Level	Interpretation question 2
2	• Developed analysis of the provenance of the two interpretations. • Differences in the provenance (e.g. time of writing, place, circumstances, audience) are explained with relevant facts/understanding. 3–4 marks
1	• Simple analysis of the provenance of the interpretation(s). • Differences in the provenance (e.g. time of writing, place, circumstances, audience) are named. 1–2 marks

Level	Interpretation question 3
4	• Complex evaluation of the two interpretations. • Argument about which interpretation is more/less convincing is shown throughout the answer, supported by relevant facts/understanding. 7–8 marks
3	• Developed evaluation of the two interpretations. • Argument is stated about which interpretation is more/less convincing. Answer is supported by relevant facts/understanding. 5–6 marks
2	• Simple answer of one interpretation (there may be a basic analysis of the other interpretation). • Answer is supported with relevant facts/understanding. 3–4 marks
1	• Basic answer on one or two interpretations. • Some facts/understanding are shown. 1–2 marks

Level	Describe question
2	• Answer explains relevant facts and understanding. 3–4 marks
1	• Answer names some relevant facts. 1–2 marks

Level	In what ways question
4	• Complex explanation of two or more changes. • A range of accurate, detailed and relevant facts are shown. 7–8 marks
3	• Developed explanation of two or more changes/consequences. • A range of accurate, relevant facts are shown. 5–6 marks
2	• Simple explanation of one change. • Specific relevant facts are shown. 3–4 marks
1	• Basic explanation of change(s). • Some basic related facts are shown. 1–2 marks

Level	Bullet points question
4	• Complex explanation of two bullet points. • A range of accurate and detailed facts that are relevant to the question. 10–12 marks
3	• Developed explanation of two bullet points. • A range of accurate facts shown that are relevant to the question. 7–9 marks
2	• Simple explanation of one or two bullet points. • Specific facts shown that are relevant to the question. 4–6 marks
1	• Basic explanation of one or two bullet points. • Some basic facts shown that are relevant to the question. 1–3 marks

America 1920–1973 Timeline

The colours represent different types of event as follows:

 Blue: economic events   Red: political events

 Black: international events or foreign policy   Yellow: social events

1920 **January** – Prohibition introduced (lasts until 1933)

1924 **June** – The Ford Motor Company sells its 10 millionth Model T

1927 **August** – Sacco and Vanzetti are executed

1927 **October** – The first ever 'talking film' is released – *The Jazz Singer*

1929 **October** – The Wall Street Crash kickstarts the Great Depression

1932 **November** – Democrat Franklin D Roosevelt (FDR) defeats President Hoover in the presidential election

1933 **March** – FDR's New Deal begins

1941 **December** – Pearl Harbor is attacked by Japanese forces; the USA declares war on Japan, officially entering the Second World War

1945 **April** – President Roosevelt dies; Vice-President Harry S Truman succeeds him

1945 **August** – The USA drops two nuclear bombs on the Japanese cities of Hiroshima and Nagasaki, leading to the end of the Second World War

1952 **November** – General Dwight D Eisenhower becomes president

1954 **May** – Racial segregation in schools is declared illegal after 'Brown v the Board of Education of Topeka' court case

1955 **December** – Rosa Parks refuses to give up her seat on the bus, leading to Montgomery Bus Boycott

1960 **November** – John F Kennedy becomes president

1963 **August** – Martin Luther King delivers his famous 'I have a dream' speech

1963 **November** – President Kennedy is assassinated; succeeded by Lyndon B Johnson

1964 **June** – The Civil Rights Act is passed, banning discrimination in jobs, voting and housing

1964 **August** – North Vietnamese boats attack two US warships, sparking escalation of the conflict in Vietnam

1973 **January** – US Supreme Court rules in 'Roe v Wade' case that women have a right to an abortion

 **RECAP**

American politics and society

The United States of America has a **constitution**, describing how the country should be governed. There are *two* types of government in the USA.

American government

Central federal government

- Based in the capital, Washington DC.
- Run by the president (elected every four years), a cabinet of advisors, and Congress (like a parliament), which is made up of elected people from the different states.
- Oversees matters that affect the whole country (like foreign affairs, the army and the postal service).

Washington DC

State government

- Based in the capital city of each state.
- Each state has its own laws, police and court system, and its own governor in charge.

For example, Austin is the state capital of Texas

Political parties in the USA

After gaining independence in 1776, voters had two main political parties to choose from.

The **Republican Party**

- More likely to preserve traditions and stay out of people's lives wherever possible (a policy called **'laissez-faire'**).
- Didn't support high taxes, which pleased many rich and business people.
- Had more support in the industrial, richer North.
- More conservative (traditional).

The **Democratic Party**

- More of an 'ordinary people's' party, preferring to intervene in everyday life if necessary.
- Favoured helping the most vulnerable, such as the poor or elderly.
- Had more support in the poorer Southern states.
- More liberal (prepared to change things – and accept change).

The Bill of Rights

The Bill of Rights is part of the constitution. It guarantees Americans a series of freedoms and rights, including the right to vote, and freedom of belief, freedom of information and freedom in law. However, by 1919, many states refused to recognise the right to vote of women, African-Americans and American Indians.

American people and society

America has a long history of immigration. By the early 1900s, there were over 100 different nationalities living there in a population of nearly 110 million. Immigration had made the USA a 'melting pot' of different races, cultures and religions.

The first Americans

- Also known as American Indians or 'Red Indians'.
- Lived in tribes across America for thousands of years before white Europeans settled there.
- The white settlers took much of their land and forced them to live in **reservations**.
- By 1900, there were only about 250,000 American Indians, down from 5 million when Europeans first arrived.

New immigrants

- A wave of new immigrants flooded into America from about 1850 onwards.
- Mainly from eastern and southern Europe, but also from Ireland, China, Japan and South America.
- Many were poor and illiterate. They crowded into the large industrial towns and cities looking for work.
- Some WASPs saw new immigrants as a threat to their way of life.

American society

Early immigrants

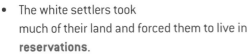

- White settlers began to arrive from Europe in the 1600s, particularly from Britain, the Netherlands and Germany.
- These settlers fought many wars between themselves and with the American Indians.
- The largest group of white settlers, the British, began to regard America as part of the British Empire. They eventually rebelled against British rule and gained their independence.
- By the 1900s, white English-speakers had become the most powerful group in America. They tended to hold the best jobs and have the most money and political power.
- About 10 per cent of American people owned 90 per cent of the wealth. They were mostly descendants of white immigrants with high status and influence, and were commonly known as WASPs (White Anglo-Saxon Protestants).

African-Americans

- Millions of Africans were taken to work as slaves in the South of America between 1600 and 1800.
- Slavery had ended in 1865, and by 1920, there were about 10 million African-Americans, mostly in the Southern states.
- Most had limited freedom, including no right to vote. They were denied access to good jobs, decent housing and proper education.
- In the early 1920s, African-Americans were among the poorest people in the country.

⚙ APPLY

DESCRIBE

a Write a sentence to explain:

- American constitution
- Bill of Rights
- Republican Party
- Democratic Party.

b Outline the similarities and differences between central and state government.

c ◉ EXAM QUESTION Describe two features of the US constitution.

 EXAMINER TIP

In 'describe' questions, it is important not to spend too long describing all you know about something. Just spend 5 minutes describing *two* features in detail.

The economic 'boom'

If a country enters a period when the vast majority of businesses are doing well, sales are high, wages increase and unemployment is low, it is usually described as a time of 'economic boom'. This happened in America during the 1920s due to a combination of reasons.

The First World War

- The USA stayed out of the war at first, following a policy of isolationism. This allowed the USA to prosper financially; American banks loaned money to Britain and its allies to buy food, weapons and equipment, mainly from the USA. This created many jobs for Americans.
- The war disrupted the economic growth of the countries that were fighting. By the end of the war the USA led the world in the production of medicines, dyes and other materials, and many basic goods.
- Nations such as France, Germany, Russia and Britain were exhausted by the end of war. Skilled American inventors and business people were now able to exploit the USA's resources and make fortunes from them.
- America was the only major nation without huge wartime debts.

The role of the Republican government

To help American businesses, the Republican government introduced several new policies:

- The Fordney-McCumber Tariff put high taxes on imports, making foreign goods more expensive. As a result, Americans bought more US-made goods, creating more jobs for Americans.
- The Republican government cut taxes paid by rich people (and their companies). As a result, the rich invested more money to start more businesses, creating more jobs.
- Taxes were low in general, so people had more money to spend.
- The Republicans' 'laissez-faire' approach meant that businesses were left alone to get on with creating wealth.

The consumer society

- The number of US homes with electricity grew rapidly in the 1920s, from 15 per cent in 1916 to nearly 70 per cent in 1927.
- This meant that people could buy ultra-modern electric-powered 'gadgets' such as vacuum cleaners, gramophones (record players), radios, telephones and refrigerators.
- Huge demand for these goods created jobs in the factories that made them.

Growing industries and mass production

- The growth of the motor industry boosted the US economy. Car-making used large quantities of US steel, leather, rubber and glass. More jobs were created in these industries as more cars were made.
- Many American businesses used the mass production methods developed in the motor industry. As companies got quicker at manufacturing, their goods became cheaper.

REVIEW

To remind yourself about the policy of 'laissez-faire', see page 12.

New ways to buy and sell

- Colourful billboards, newspapers and magazines urged people to buy the latest gadgets and keep up with their neighbours. This led to a boost in sales.

- Catalogues made buying easy, and the goods could be delivered to your door.
- 'Buy now, pay later' schemes (sometimes called '**hire purchase plans**') meant buyers could pay for goods in small instalments over a fixed period. Six out of ten cars were bought this way.

This diagram shows how America's economic boom kept going in a 'cycle of prosperity':

- Mass production means that goods can be made a lot more cheaply
- More people can afford to buy goods
- More people are employed to make these goods
- People spend their wages on more goods
- Advertising persuades people to buy even more goods
- Hire purchase plans help people buy goods

Cycle of prosperity

REVISION SKILLS

Mnemonics are usually words or phrases formed from the first letters of key words. They are useful memory devices that can help you recall lists of causes and consequences, a sequence of events, or actions. Identify the key words for the topic. Write them out, then rearrange them so that the initial letters spell something you can remember. For example, a mnemonic for this topic could be:

Afford   **S**pend   **H**ire (purchase)

Advertising   **M**ass (production)   **E**mployed

= ASHAME

Sales of **consumer goods** grew hugely during the 1920s. By 1929, America made nearly half of all the world's consumer goods.

Cars
1919: 9 million
1929: 26 million

Radios
1919: 60,000
1929: 10 million

Telephones
1919: 10 million
1929: 20 million

Refrigerators
For every refrigerator in 1921, there were 167 by 1929

EXAMINER TIP

You must write about at least two ways in which ordinary people's lives were affected.

APPLY

IN WHAT WAYS

a Define the following terms:
- economic boom
- consumer society.

b Copy and complete the table:

Reasons for America's boom	Two facts about this reason	How did this reason contribute to the economic boom?
First World War		
New consumer goods		
Mass production		
Advertising		
'Buy now, pay later' schemes		
Import duties		
Low taxes		
'Laissez-faire'		

c **EXAM QUESTION** In what ways did the lives of ordinary Americans change as a result of the economic boom in the USA during the 1920s?

Henry Ford and the motor industry

The Ford Motor Company

- The first Ford factory was built in 1903 in Detroit, Michigan.
- By 1913, Ford introduced a new method of production – the assembly line – which meant the cars could be made quicker and cheaper.
- Ford's assembly line used an electric conveyor belt that carried the partly assembled car past workers who did one or two small jobs repeatedly, such as fitting wheels or doors.
- Ford's Model T car was mass produced on the assembly line.
- As production got quicker, the price of the car fell. Costing nearly $800 in 1911, by 1928 it was only $295. 15 million people bought Model Ts between 1911 and 1929.

The impact of the boom in the motor industry

- For every worker in a car factory, there were ten more making the parts that the cars needed.
- There were also jobs building roads, highways and oil refineries to supply the fuel as well as in petrol stations, roadside hotels, garages and restaurants.
- There were social changes:
  - ➤ Positive – car owners felt a new sense of freedom. People no longer had to live near offices and factories. They could buy a house out of town and drive into work.
  - ➤ Negative – traffic jams, accidents and pollution.

The Ford Model T

- The Model T was slow, considered ugly by some, and hard to drive, but sturdy, very reliable and built with easy-to-change parts.
- It was the right product at the right time, catching the public imagination when they were desperate for new gadgets and a chance to go beyond their own backyards. Ford called his Model T 'an affordable car for ordinary people', and it changed the motor industry forever.
- By 1926, there were nearly 20 million cars on America's roads, and one in two was a Ford.

The stock market boom

One of the biggest success stories of the 1920s – and one of the most popular ways to make money – was the buying and selling of shares in companies. This was often called 'playing the **stock market**'.

How does the stock market work?

1. To set up a company you need money for wages, equipment, land and so on.

2. Most companies get money from investors. In return, investors own a share of the company – they become shareholders.

3. A shareholder makes money by:

   i. receiving a share of the company profits – a dividend – each year

   ii. selling their share for a higher price than they paid for it – if the company does well and makes good profits, its shares become more valuable. But a shareholder might not be able to sell their share if the company is doing badly – a shareholder could be stuck with a share no one wants to buy and pays no dividends!

Playing the stock market

- During the 1920s, millions of ordinary Americans, not just the rich, bought shares in all sorts of companies and made money by selling them on.

- In 1920, there were only 4 million people who owned shares. By 1929, there were five times as many.
- Many people bought shares with money borrowed from banks or with a small deposit of 10 per cent. They would then pay the remaining amount with the profits they made when the shares were sold. This method of purchasing shares was called '**buying on the margin**'.

REVIEW

The wealth created by both the development of the motor industry and the stock market contributed to the economic boom you examined on pages 14 and 15.

APPLY

DESCRIBE

a Define the following terms in no more than 15 words:

- stock market
- investor
- shareholder
- dividend
- 'buying on the margin'.

b   **EXAM QUESTION** Describe two ways in which an investor might make money from 'playing the stock market'.

EXAMINER TIP

Understanding the meanings of these important terms would be useful in helping you to answer a 'describe' question on how people made a profit on the stock market.

INTERPRETATION ANALYSIS

a What new method of production did Henry Ford use in his factory?

b Look at these interpretations of working for Henry Ford.

▼ **INTERPRETATION A** *Red Cole, a production worker who joined Ford aged 18, interviewed in 1995 BBC documentary* People's Century: On the line:

> The thing about Mr Ford that stuck in my mind was that he started to pay $5 a day. And that Mr Ford was like a God because he had control of so many thousands of people and had them in such order – the production lines, the coming and going, three shifts, eight hours each shift – days, afternoons and midnights – and everything to me was like clockwork and I was so proud to be a part of it.

▼ **INTERPRETATION B** *Adapted from a 1969 biography of Ford by Booton Herndon, an award-winning reporter; Harry Bennett was Ford's second in command:*

> Bennett liked boxers and wrestlers, and many, particularly the big tough ones, ended up on the payroll. He sought out tough cops and hired them. He built up a small army of thugs who kept the workers under complete control. Anyone doing anything naughty, like talking union, was beaten to a pulp and fired.

c   **EXAM QUESTION**

1 How does **Interpretation B** differ from **Interpretation A** about working at Ford? Explain your answer using **Interpretations A** and **B**.

2 Why might the authors of **Interpretations A** and **B** have a different interpretation about working at Ford? Explain your answer using **Interpretations A** and **B** and your contextual knowledge.

EXAMINER TIP

Consider what it would be like for the Ford workers if Interpretation B is true.

The inequalities of wealth in the 1920s

The 1920s was not a time of economic prosperity for all Americans. Millions of people remained poor, particularly those in rural areas or who worked in older, more traditional industries.

- America was a place where wealth was spread very unequally. The richest 5 per cent earned 33 per cent of all the money.
- There were an estimated 15,000 US millionaires in 1927. In contrast, 6 million families – 42 per cent of the total – had an income of less than $1000 a year, which meant they could not buy basic necessities such as decent food and good quality housing.
- Many large industrial firms were able to keep their profits high by paying low wages to their unskilled workers.

 REVIEW

To remind yourself of how the USA had benefited from the First World War, look back at page 14.

Poverty in the countryside

Many of America's rural areas saw increasing levels of poverty in the 1920s. By the early 1930s, farmers were only earning a third of their income in 1920. There were several reasons for this:

- After the First World War, there was less demand in Europe for American imports.
- Some countries taxed US products, making them expensive and difficult to sell to customers overseas.
- The use of high-tech farming machinery produced more food to sell. Prices fell, and farmers became poorer as a result.
- Some farmers had borrowed money from the banks to buy the latest machinery and now they could not repay the loans. As a result, many farmers were forced to sell their farms to raise money or were evicted from their land.
- Around 600,000 farmers lost their farms in 1924 alone. The farm workers also lost their jobs.

Problems in traditional industries

Some industries that were once prosperous were overtaken by new rival industries:

- Coal miners suffered because coal mines closed. Other forms of fuel (oil, gas and electricity) were increasingly used to heat homes and cook food.
- Cotton and wool factory workers suffered – there was less demand for their products because of the popularity of new man-made fibres, such as rayon, and fashions for shorter dresses, which required less material. The price of cotton and woollen cloth fell and many factories shut down.

African-American workers

Most African-Americans lived in the Southern states, such as Mississippi and South Carolina. They were hit hard in the 1920s.

- Many worked on farms as labourers or were **sharecroppers** who rented small areas of farmland from a landowner.
- As the farming industry suffered in general, African-American farmworkers and sharecroppers were hit particularly hard because they were already desperately poor.
- Many moved to cities to work but could often only find low-paid jobs.

American Indians

Life was also very hard for most of the original inhabitants of the country, the American Indians.

- Large amounts of their land had been seized by mining companies and much of their traditional way of life had been lost.
- Many American Indians had been forced to move to reservations. Often, the soil there was so poor that it was impossible to grow crops properly.
- Most American Indians lived in extreme poverty, were poorly educated and had a lower life expectancy than other ethnic groups in US society.

SUMMARY

- Immigration had made the USA a very multiracial society. By the 1900s, the descendants of white European settlers had become the most powerful group in America.

- During the 1920s, because of a combination of different reasons, America experienced an economic boom.

- The development of the motor industry and the growth of the stock market were two of the best-known examples of this boom.

- But the 1920s was not a time of economic prosperity for all – millions remained poor, particularly in rural areas or those who worked in traditional industries.

APPLY

DESCRIBE

a Write a definition for the term 'inequalities of wealth'. Use examples in your definition.

b Make a set of revision cards that summarises the inequalities of wealth in America in the 1920s. Make sure you have a card on each of the following:

- Facts about rich America and poor America
- Poverty in the countryside
- Declining traditional industries
- Poverty among African-Americans
- Poverty among American Indians.

c **EXAM QUESTION** Describe the problem of poverty faced by two groups of people in America in the 1920s.

EXAMINER TIP

You should spend around 5 minutes on this question and your answer should be factual.

CHAPTER 2

Social and cultural developments

 **RECAP**

The Roaring Twenties

The 1920s were a time of great social and cultural change. For many Americans, it was a decade of having fun and enjoying loud music, wild parties and new forms of entertainment. Millions of people had more money and more leisure time than ever before and were determined to make the most of it. This time in US history is often called the 'Roaring Twenties'.

Jazz music

The 1920s is sometimes referred to as the 'Jazz Age' because a new form of music – **jazz** – became incredibly popular.

- Jazz originated in the Southern states of America among African-Americans and spread north as African-Americans began to move in search of work.
- It is known for improvisation, fast tempos and lively rhythms.
- The loud, lively music appealed to the young, both black and white. It soon became the most popular musical style in dancehalls, bars and nightclubs in big Northern cities such as Chicago and New York.
- Jazz provided great opportunities for black musicians such as Louis Armstrong, Duke Ellington and Bessie Smith.
- New dance crazes became popular, like the Charleston, the One Step, the Tango and the Black Bottom.
- Some people criticised jazz, particularly the older generation. They felt that it encouraged drunkenness and that the dances were too sexual.

Cinema

The movie industry grew rapidly in the 1920s.

- Many of the major movie companies built studios in Hollywood, an area just outside the Californian city of Los Angeles, because it enjoyed year-round sunshine.
- Weekly audiences grew from 35 million in 1919 to 100 million in 1930.
- Studios introduced the 'star system' to promote their main actors. They made sure that the media had full access to the star, making them do magazine interviews, photo shoots, appear on radio shows and make public appearances.
- Charlie Chaplin, Rudolf Valentino and Clara Bow became household names at this time.

- By 1929, Hollywood film studios were making over 500 films a year, giving employment to thousands and entertainment to millions.
- *The Jazz Singer* was released in 1927 – the first feature-length film to include sound (known as a 'talkie').

However, the movies horrified many older Americans. They worried about the sexual content of some films and the impact this was having on the young. When several states threatened to ban films, Hollywood introduced the Hays Code – a list of strict rules, which included a ban on nudity.

Sport

The 1920s was a golden age for American sport.

- Sportspeople, such as Babe Ruth (baseball) and Bobby Jones (golf) became celebrities. By 1930, Ruth was earning $80,000 a year, the equivalent of nearly £7 million a year today.
- Radio broadcasts, newspapers and magazines helped bring major sporting events to a mass audience.

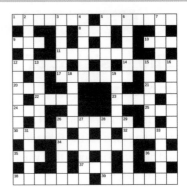

Crazy crazes

The Roaring Twenties was a time of crazes. The following all became very popular for a short period of time:

- A Chinese board game called Mahjong
- Crossword puzzles
- Marathon dancing and pole sitting (people would see how long they could dance, or sit on top of a pole, without stopping or falling off).

 **APPLY**

INTERPRETATION ANALYSIS

▼ **INTERPRETATION A** *Jelly Roll Morton (1890–1941) was an American jazz pianist, bandleader and composer from New Orleans, Louisiana. Here he speaks shortly before his death about the time his grandmother found out he was playing in a jazz band in his teenage years:*

> When my grandmother found out that I was playing jazz in one of the sporting houses in the district, she told me that I had disgraced the family and forbade me to live at the house. She told me that devil music would surely bring about my downfall, but I just couldn't put it behind me.

a Summarise what Jelly Roll Morton's grandmother said about jazz music.

b Can you suggest reasons why she felt this way?

 REVIEW

For top tips on how to approach the 'interpretation' questions, take a look at the guidance on pages 7 and 8.

DESCRIBE

a Copy and complete this table, writing two facts about the new and exciting developments in each of these types of entertainment during the 1920s.

Entertainment	Fact 1	Fact 2
Jazz music		
Cinema		
Sport		
Crazes		

b Why do you think this decade in US history is often referred to as the 'Roaring Twenties'?

c

 EXAM QUESTION Describe two new developments in American entertainment in the 1920s.

 EXAMINER TIP

Make a quick decision when answering 'describe' questions. Here, choose 'sport' and 'cinema', for example, and then write down several facts about the way they developed in the 1920s.

REVISION SKILLS

Record yourself reading your notes. Playing back the information when you are travelling or waiting will help you absorb it more easily.

The position of women in society

Life changed for millions of American women in the 1920s. Many had jobs for the first time and were wearing clothes and behaving in ways that would have been unthinkable a decade before.

Women before the war

- Most women led restricted lives and could not vote.
- Middle- and upper-class women were expected to behave politely at all times and wear sensible clothing. They rarely played energetic sport and wore little make-up. Relationships with men were strictly controlled.
- For poorer women who had to work, there were few opportunities for promotion. They usually had to settle for poorly paid jobs such as cleaning, low-skilled factory work and secretarial work.

Women during the First World War

The war brought important changes for women:

- Women took over the jobs of the men who went away to fight.
- They worked just as hard and as well as men and the money they earned gave them a sense of independence.
- American women were given the right to vote in 1920, partly as a result of their war work.
- By 1929, there were around 10.5 million women with jobs, around 25 per cent more than in 1920.

Changing lives

With money of their own, and the sense of independence they had experienced during the war, many women began to make more of their own decisions about how they lived.

> More women lived on their own.

> They were less likely to stay in an unhappy marriage – the divorce rate doubled during the 1920s.

> **How did the lives of some women change?**

> Some women began to behave and dress differently – wearing more revealing clothes and smoking and drinking in public, for example.

> A survey in 1900 showed that nearly 80 per cent of college students questioned had not had sex before marriage. A similar survey in 1920 found that only 31 per cent had not had sex before marriage.

What was a 'flapper'?

The independent and fashionable young women of the 1920s were often described as 'flappers'.

- Mainly middle- and upper-class women from the Northern states.
- Some rode motorbikes and went to nightclubs with men until the early hours of the morning.
- Their liberal attitude shocked more traditional members of society, who saw flappers as an example of the evils of modern life and felt that family life, religion and traditional values were under threat.
- An Anti-Flirt League was formed to protest against the flappers' behaviour.

Change for the better?

Life did not change for all American women. For most, especially those in the South and rural areas, life went on as before. Women worked and raised their families, and did not have enough income to buy luxuries. Despite gaining the vote, women were still not equal to men. Women worked in low-skilled jobs and earned less than men in the same job.

REVIEW

The position of women in the 1920s mirrors US society in general in the 1920s; for some, life changed a lot – but for others, life continued as it had done for many years.

SUMMARY

- Great social and cultural changes took place in America in the 1920s.

- Jazz music became incredibly popular.

- The movie industry grew rapidly.

- Life changed for millions of American women; many had jobs for the first time and began wearing different and daring clothes.

- Flappers were the independent and fashionable young women of the 1920s. They were mainly middle- and upper-class women from the Northern states.

- However, for millions of women in the Southern states and poorer, rural areas, life didn't change significantly.

APPLY

IN WHAT WAYS

a Define the term 'flapper'.

b Write three facts under each of the following headings:

- Women before the First World War
- Women during the war
- Women after the war

c Did life change for *all* American women in the 1920s? Explain your answer.

d **EXAM QUESTION** In what ways did the lives of some American women change in the 1920s?

EXAMINER TIP

The best answers will not just include what life was like in the 1920s, they will briefly explain what life was like for women *before* 1920 as well.

BULLET POINTS

EXAM QUESTION Which of the following had more impact on America in the 1920s:

- Cultural changes
- Social changes?

EXAMINER TIP

Use the cultural changes explained on pages 20–21 and the social changes affecting women on these pages to help you with your answer.

CHAPTER 3

Divided society

Prohibition

Prohibition was the nationwide ban on the production, importation, transportation and sale of alcohol from 1920 to 1933. There were several reasons why Prohibition was introduced:

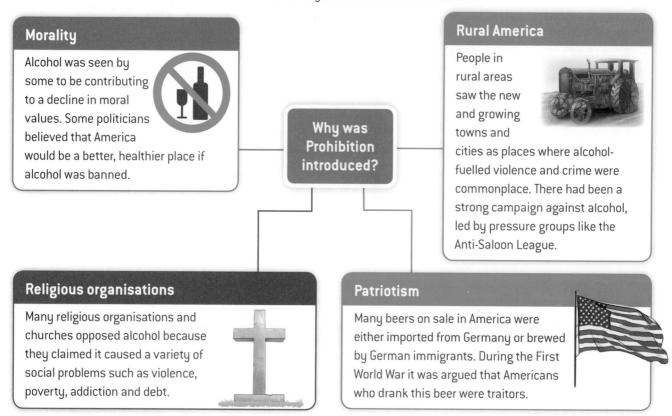

Morality

Alcohol was seen by some to be contributing to a decline in moral values. Some politicians believed that America would be a better, healthier place if alcohol was banned.

Why was Prohibition introduced?

Rural America

People in rural areas saw the new and growing towns and cities as places where alcohol-fuelled violence and crime were commonplace. There had been a strong campaign against alcohol, led by pressure groups like the Anti-Saloon League.

Religious organisations

Many religious organisations and churches opposed alcohol because they claimed it caused a variety of social problems such as violence, poverty, addiction and debt.

Patriotism

Many beers on sale in America were either imported from Germany or brewed by German immigrants. During the First World War it was argued that Americans who drank this beer were traitors.

Around 1500 'Prohibition agents' tried to enforce the law. They tried to locate places that sold or made alcohol, then make arrests and confiscate the alcohol. However:

- The USA has 18,600 miles of coastline and land borders to patrol. The agents faced a near impossible task of trying to prevent alcohol being smuggled in by sea or over the border (known as 'bootlegging') from Mexico in the South or Canada in the North.
- Millions of people were willing to break the law and continue drinking, so Prohibition was difficult to enforce.
- It was very easy to get alcohol because criminal gangs got involved in making and supplying it. These gangs ran illegal bars ('speakeasies'), which sold bootleg alcohol. They also sold moonshine – a home-made spirit. Speakeasies were hidden in cellars or private hotel rooms.
- The gangs made so much money that they were able to avoid arrest and prosecution because they bribed some of the police officers, Prohibition agents, border guards and judges.

Organised crime

The gangs did not just get involved in the illegal alcohol trade. They also made money through fixing horse and dog racing, running brothels and racketeering (when businessmen paid money to the gangs to stop them smashing up their premises). A new phrase was coined to describe this behaviour – **organised crime**. Some of the best-known 'gangsters' were Al Capone (who made $10 million a year from racketeering alone), 'Lucky' Luciano, 'Machine Gun' Kelly and Vito 'Chicken Head' Gurino.

At the height of his power, Al 'Scarface' Capone was making $2 million a week through organised crime, which he ran like a business.

Organised crime leaders were rarely arrested or charged with any offences because they had a great deal of control over the police. Also, no witnesses ever wanted to come forward against them.

The impact of Prohibition on society

By 1933, it was clear that Prohibition was not working. There were approximately 200,000 speakeasies in the USA. In New York, there were more speakeasies than there were bars before Prohibition. Instead of America becoming a less violent, more honest and moral country, it had seen the rise of gangsters, organised crime and police corruption.

- The Association Against the Prohibition Amendment (AAPA) attracted thousands of members. They argued that Prohibition was a threat to a person's right to choose to drink and that Prohibition was making people lose respect for the law.
- It was argued that if alcohol was legalised again, lots of legal jobs would be created in the brewing industry.
- The government could also tax the alcohol itself, so the government would make money rather than the gangsters.

In the 1932 presidential election campaign, Franklin D Roosevelt gained many votes because he opposed Prohibition. He won the election, and in early 1933 he repealed (got rid of) Prohibition.

 **APPLY**

IN WHAT WAYS

a Write no more than 10 words to describe each of the following:

- Prohibition
- bootlegging
- speakeasy
- moonshine
- organised crime
- gangster.

b Make two lists. One list should contain reasons why Prohibition was introduced, the other should contain reasons why it failed.

c **EXAM QUESTION** In what ways did Prohibition change US society?

 EXAMINER TIP

Remember that the question is *not* asking you to define Prohibition, or outline why it was introduced – the question simply asks that you write about the ways in which Prohibition *changed* US society.

REVISION SKILLS

Create a 10-point fact quiz to test detailed knowledge about a topic. You could swap the test with a friend.

Immigration

Between 1850 and 1914, around 40 million people emigrated to America.

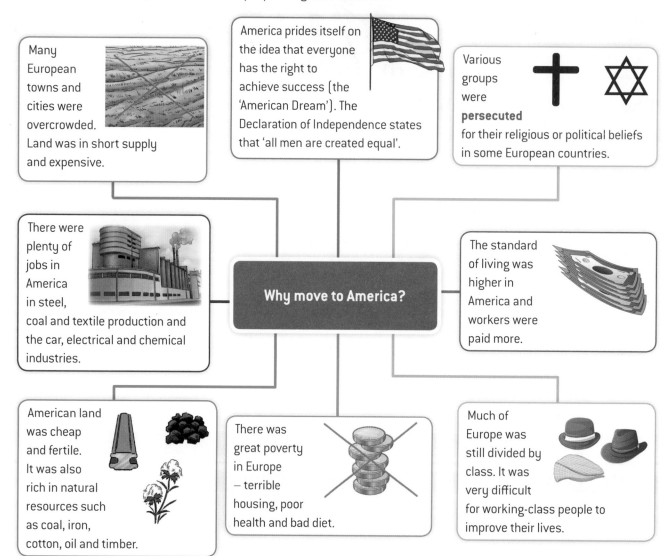

Many European towns and cities were overcrowded. Land was in short supply and expensive.

America prides itself on the idea that everyone has the right to achieve success (the 'American Dream'). The Declaration of Independence states that 'all men are created equal'.

Various groups were **persecuted** for their religious or political beliefs in some European countries.

There were plenty of jobs in America in steel, coal and textile production and the car, electrical and chemical industries.

Why move to America?

The standard of living was higher in America and workers were paid more.

American land was cheap and fertile. It was also rich in natural resources such as coal, iron, cotton, oil and timber.

There was great poverty in Europe – terrible housing, poor health and bad diet.

Much of Europe was still divided by class. It was very difficult for working-class people to improve their lives.

The impact of immigration

- In the late 1800s and early 1900s, more immigrants began to arrive from southern and eastern Europe.
- Large ethnic communities developed in many larger cities (Little Italy in New York, for example).
- In some cities these immigrants were often resented because they were usually poor, couldn't speak English well and had unfamiliar traditions and religious practices. Many were Jewish or Catholic, whereas most of the established population was Protestant.
- The First World War had added to American suspicion of 'foreigners'. Further, in the Russian Revolution of 1917, citizens had risen up and taken over land, banks and businesses. Some Americans feared that Russian immigrants might try something similar.

The immigrant experience

- Some immigrants achieved great success, opening thriving businesses and making a good living.
- However, for many, working and living conditions were generally very poor and difficult.
- Many immigrants were poorly educated and willing to work for very low wages in any kind of job.
- Consequently, some felt that the immigrants were out to 'steal' jobs, which created prejudice.

Immigration laws

The government began introducing new laws that limited the number of new arrivals.

A 1917 law (sometimes called the Literacy Act) banned entry to any immigrant over the age of 16 who could not read a sentence of 40 words.

1921 Immigration Quota Law: allowed only 350,000 immigrants to enter each year.

1924 National Origins Act: allowed only 150,000 immigrants to enter each year.

APPLY

INTERPRETATION ANALYSIS

a Look at these two interpretations about being an immigrant in America.

▼ **INTERPRETATION A** *Miguel Santos, an immigrant to New York from Cuba, interviewed in 1940 for the Federal Writers' Project, a US government scheme. He was speaking about his experience soon after arriving in New York in 1904:*

> Do you want to know the truth? The word 'liberty' is heard a lot in the USA. So how come, when we come here, do we have to stick together because of the hatred Americans feel towards us? They get drunk and they pick a quarrel. I said to one of them, 'Why do you talk to me in this contemptuous [insulting] way?' and he closes his hand to threaten me. So, I threw the first punch, and this policeman comes to arrest me. And you talk about 'democracy' and the 'rights of man'!

▼ **INTERPRETATION B** *Louis Adamic emigrated from Slovenia in 1913 and settled in California. He wrote the following in his book,* Laughing in the Jungle, *published in 1932 describing what he had been told about America:*

> My notion of the United States is that it was a grand, amazing, fantastic place – the Golden country, huge beyond conception, untellably exciting.
>
> In America one could make pots of money in a short time, acquire immense holdings [land and property], wear a white collar and have polish on one's boots – and eat white bread, soup and meat on weekdays as well as on Sundays, even if you were an ordinary workman.

b Briefly sum up what the two men think of America. Which words do they use to show their feelings?

c

 EXAM QUESTION

1 How does **Interpretation B** differ from **Interpretation A** about the immigrant experience in America in the 1920s? Explain your answer using **Interpretations A** and **B**.

2 Why might the authors of **Interpretations A** and **B** have a different interpretation of the immigrant experience in America in the 1920s? Explain your answer using **Interpretations A** and **B** and your contextual knowledge.

DESCRIBE

a Suggest reasons why some immigrants faced problems establishing a life for themselves in America.

b How did America try to cut immigration?

c

 EXAM QUESTION Describe two problems faced by immigrants to America in the 1920s.

EXAMINER TIP

Make sure you describe both problems in roughly equal detail – don't spend too long on one or the other.

REVIEW

Look back at page 13 to remind yourself of the different immigrant groups who were already settled in the USA at this time.

Racial tension

- Slavery was abolished in the USA in 1865, but by this time there were more black people than white in the South.
- White politicians, often driven by racial prejudice and fear, tried to keep control by passing laws (known as 'Jim Crow Laws') to keep African-Americans **segregated**.
- African-Americans were stopped from using the same restaurants, hotels, swimming pools and even cemeteries as white people. Ways were found to stop them voting.
- African-Americans were segregated in the military, and some states banned mixed-race marriages.
- African-Americans could not expect justice from the legal system, because many judges, sheriffs and police upheld the Jim Crow Laws.

Leaving the South

Many African-Americans left the Southern states and headed north, attracted by better pay and opportunities in the new industries. The African-American population of Chicago and New York more than doubled in the early 1900s. However, there was still racism:

African-Americans were often the last to be hired and the first to be fired.	They occupied the worst housing in the poorest areas of the cities.	Some factories only employed white workers or paid black workers the lowest wages.	There were occasional race riots – in 1919, for example, after a black youth accidentally entered a 'whites only' beach in Chicago.

REVIEW

Millions of African-Americans from the Southern states were attracted to the North as a result of the booming industries there – see pages 14–16.

The black 'Renaissance'

- Some African-American communities flourished in the Northern cities.
- Harlem, a neighbourhood of New York, became a centre for creativity, black culture and black pride when talented black poets, writers, artists and musicians gathered there. Some called this the black 'Renaissance'.
- White customers were attracted to these areas by the excitement and liveliness of the new nightclubs and jazz bars.
- Some African-Americans even entered politics. In 1910, WEB Du Bois – the great-grandson of an African slave – set up the NAACP, the National Association for the Advancement of Colored People, which worked to improve the rights of African-Americans, such as campaigning for the right to vote.

The Ku Klux Klan

What was the KKK?

A racist terror group with a membership of around 5 million in 1925.

What were its aims?

Maintain white supremacy over African-Americans and immigrants and 'keep them in their place'.

How did it start?

Founded in the 1860s to terrorise African-Americans in the Southern states. Black people were beaten up or even killed in the hope that they would be too scared to register to vote. The original KKK declined towards the end of the nineteenth century.

The Klan becomes popular again

A 1915 Hollywood feature film, *The Birth of a Nation*, showed Klansmen saving white families from violent black criminals. The film glorified the Klan as an organisation that protected decent, law-abiding citizens. It attracted huge audiences and sparked a revival; by 1925, KKK membership had reached around 5 million.

- Most members were poor white people, mainly from rural areas of Southern and Western states.
- They looked for someone to blame for their poverty, and turned on not just African-Americans, but also Jewish people, Catholics and immigrants. They felt that black and immigrant workers' willingness to work for lower wages took jobs from white people.
- The Klan was against anyone that wasn't like them – white and Protestant. They saw themselves as 'defenders' of their Protestant religion and against what they saw as a decline in moral standards. They attacked drunks and gamblers to 'clean up' society.
- The secrecy of the Klan, with its coded language, menacing hooded costume and strange rituals, was part of the appeal for many men who joined.

KKK methods

Dressed in white sheets, white hoods and carrying US flags, their methods of violence and intimidation included whipping, branding with acid, kidnapping, castration and **lynching**.

The decline of the Klan

In 1925, a popular local Klan leader was convicted of the brutal kidnapping, rape and murder of a young woman. At his trial, he exposed many of the secrets of the KKK. He was sentenced to life imprisonment and, within a year, KKK membership had fallen from 5 million to 300,000.

APPLY

IN WHAT WAYS

a In no more than 15 words, define the following terms:

- segregation
- Jim Crow Laws
- black 'Renaissance'.

b Why was the KKK so popular in the early 1920s?

c
> **EXAM QUESTION** In what ways did the lives of African-Americans change in the 1920s?

EXAMINER TIP

It is important that you show that there were both benefits and problems for African-Americans in the 1920s.

Rising fear of immigrants

- Some saw immigrants as an enemy who brought 'un-American' ideas into the country.
- Communism was especially feared. Americans were concerned that a communist revolution (like the one in Russia in 1917) could happen in America – especially as America had let in nearly 1.5 million Russians in the past few years.
- An American Communist Party had been set up in 1919, and industrial unrest was increasing.
- Anarchists were another group greatly feared in the 1920s. Anarchists believe that countries should not be ruled by organised governments, but by a system where everyone rules themselves through voluntary cooperation.
- Many Americans felt they had good reason to fear anarchists – in 1901, an anarchist called Leon Franz Czolgosz had shot dead US President William McKinley.

The 'Palmer Raids' and the 'Red Scare'

- In July 1919, a bomb destroyed the house of Alexander Mitchell Palmer, the man in charge of America's law and police. A communist newspaper was found next to the body of the suicide bomber.
- Later that year, an unidentified bomber blew up 30 people in New York. No one was ever found guilty – but many people's fear of communism increased even more.
- Palmer vowed to get rid of America's communists – or 'Reds'. During the 'Palmer Raids', around 6000 suspected communists were arrested across 33 cities. Little evidence of any communist plots was found.
- This period is known as the 'Red Scare'.

Communism

In Russia in 1917, a political group called the communists (known as 'Reds') had overthrown – and later killed – their rulers. Communists:

- believe that all workers should join together, rebel against a country's ruling classes and share all wealth equally among the citizens
- are committed to the improvement of workers' rights and working conditions.

The case of Sacco and Vanzetti

Nicola Sacco and Bartolomeo Vanzetti were Italian-born immigrant anarchists who were charged with robbing a shoe factory and murdering two staff in April 1920. Their 45-day trial began in May 1921.

→

There were doubts about the evidence against them. Even Judge Webster Thayer said that Vanzetti 'may not actually have committed the crime but he is morally to blame because he is our enemy'.

↓

There was no conclusive evidence, but the jury found them guilty and sentenced them to death.

←

The pair said they were innocent. It was argued that they didn't understand what was going on because they spoke such poor English.

The importance of the case

- The trial was reported all over the world and there were huge demonstrations against the verdict.
- Protesters said the trial was unfair and the two men were found guilty as much for their race and their anarchist ideas as for their actions.
- Despite years of protests and appeals, the two men were executed by electric chair on 23 August 1927.

SUMMARY

- Prohibition was the nationwide ban on the production, importation, transportation and sale of alcohol. It lasted from 1920 to 1933.

- Prohibition was largely ignored. It was difficult to enforce, and the era saw a rise in organised crime.

- In some cities immigrants were often resented because they were usually poor, couldn't speak English well and had unfamiliar traditions and religious practices.

- Some saw immigrants as an enemy who brought 'un-American' ideas into the country.

- Communism was especially feared, leading to the Red Scare.

- 'Jim Crow Laws' kept African-Americans segregated, especially in the South, where the KKK was popular.

- Many African-Americans left the South and headed north, attracted by jobs, better pay and opportunities in the new industries.

- Today, many historians see the case of Sacco and Vanzetti as an example of just how intolerant of immigrants US society had become in the 1920s.

 APPLY

BULLET POINTS

a Make a set of revision cards for the Red Scare. Use the following headings:

- Why was there a fear of immigrants?
- The Palmer Raids
- Sacco and Vanzetti
- Red Scare summary

Jot down 3 or 4 points on each card. Try to include a factual detail with each point.

b

 EXAM QUESTION Which of the following had the greater impact on America in the 1920s:

- The Ku Klux Klan
- The Red Scare?

Explain your answer with reference to both topics.

> **EXAMINER TIP**
> Try to explain how each was seen to be fighting against a threat to American values.

CHAPTER 4

American society during the Depression

 **RECAP**

The Wall Street Crash

'Playing the stock market' was very popular in the 1920s due to the large profits that could be made. Throughout the decade, share prices constantly rose, so investors would keep their shares for a short time and then sell them on at a profit. Banks lent money to the investors knowing they would get their money back soon – with interest.

However, at the end of the decade, the stock market 'crashed'.

Inequalities of wealth

- Not all Americans could afford the goods that the factories produced.
- There was a limit to the number of cars, radios, telephones and fridges people needed and would buy.
- American factories were making goods faster than they could sell them (overproduction) and profits were beginning to fall.

Problems abroad

- Companies struggled to sell their goods abroad because foreign governments had put taxes (or tariffs) on US-made goods.
- These countries wanted to encourage their citizens to buy goods made in their own country.

Lack of confidence

- Some shareholders began to doubt whether the companies in which they had invested would keep making large profits.
- In September 1929, a few cautious people began to sell their shares, worried that they wouldn't get their portion of company profits at the end of the year.

People start to panic

- More and more people began to sell their shares as word spread about the falling profits of leading US companies.
- Shareholders realised that their shares (which were only pieces of paper entitling them to a share of company profits) were only worth something if someone was willing to buy them.
- As they tried to sell their shares for cash, they dropped their price to attract a buyer.

'Black Thursday'

- On 24 October 1929, 13 million shares were sold on the New York Stock Exchange on Wall Street – five times as many as on a normal day.
- Share prices in nearly all companies continued to drop.
- Some investors called this 'Black Thursday'; others called it the 'Crash'.

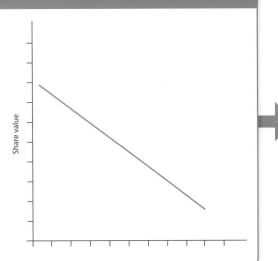

Beyond 'Black Thursday'

- People continued to try to sell their shares.
- On Tuesday 29 October, there was another mad panic to sell shares – at any price.
- 16 million shares were sold during the day and the average price of shares dropped by 40 cents.
- Shareholders lost a total of $8 billion.

Banks go bankrupt

- It wasn't just shareholders who lost money.
- Many Americans had borrowed money from banks to buy shares, hoping to pay back their loans when the shares rose in price.
- When share prices fell, investors couldn't sell their shares for enough to be able to pay their bank back in full.
- When lots of customers couldn't pay back their loans, the banks went bankrupt. In 1929 alone, 659 banks went bust.
- Some people lost all their bank savings.

APPLY

DESCRIBE

a Write definitions for the terms 'overproduction', 'foreign tariffs' and 'profit'.

b Create your own flow diagram that outlines how Wall Street crashed. Make sure you include the following:

- inequality of wealth
- overproduction
- foreign tariffs
- concern over low profits
- panic selling of shares
- Black Thursday
- 29 October 1929
- bankrupt banks.

c Describe two problems in the American economy that contributed to the Wall Street Crash.

REVIEW

Look back to pages 14 and 15 and remind yourselves why America boomed in the years after the First World War.

EXAMINER TIP

You are not being asked to explain what the Wall Street Crash was. Instead you must focus your answer on problems that existed within the US economy that led to the Crash.

REVISION SKILLS

Write topic facts on sticky notes and put them up in your bedroom or elsewhere in your house. Read your notes when you see them and you will begin to associate that part of the house with that topic, making your notes easier to remember!

The impact of the Great Depression on people's lives

By 1930, most Americans were using the term 'the **Great Depression**' to describe the effects of the Wall Street Crash. A 'depression' is when factories close, banks fail and unemployment reaches record levels.

Ordinary shareholders

- Millions of investors lost a fortune.
- They tried to pay back bank loans by selling valuables.
- Some struggled to pay rent and faced homelessness.

The very rich

- Some rich people lost part of their wealth because they had invested in shares or owned factories that closed.
- However, many owned lots of property and land and were not affected greatly.

Businessmen and their workers

- Factories had been overproducing.
- After the Crash, people had less money to spend, so fewer goods were sold (underconsumption).
- Factory owners cut production, wages, and finally, jobs.
- Closures affected local businesses too: for example, fewer workers eating at restaurants near factories meant some restaurants closed too.

Farmers

- Many farmers struggled before the Crash.
- Farmers with bank loans for equipment had to pay back the money. Some couldn't afford to pay their debts or mortgages and faced losing their farms and sacking their workers. By 1932, 1 in 20 farmers had been evicted.
- A combination of drought and poor farming methods turned the land into a 'Dust Bowl'. Huge dust storms blew away millions of acres of dry topsoil, making it impossible to farm.

Bank managers

- When banks went bust bank managers and staff lost their jobs.

Around 250,000 Americans stopped paying their mortgages in 1932 alone – most were evicted.

Some unemployed workers, known as hobos, travelled the country looking for work.

Unemployment

Around 13 million people had lost their jobs by 1932, nearly 25 per cent of the labour force.

By 1932, 12,000 people a day lost their jobs and 20,000 companies had closed.

Hobos and Hoovervilles

Many took to living on the streets. Some moved to urban waste ground and built shacks with boxes, scrap metal and old cloth. These settlements were called Hoovervilles.

The homeless queued in 'breadlines' for food from soup kitchens.

Between 1929 and 1932, factory production dropped by 45 per cent and house-building fell by 80 per cent.

President Hoover's response

- Hoover was convinced that America would recover soon.
- He believed in 'rugged individualism' – that people can overcome problems with hard work, not government help.
- However, Hoover did try to improve things:
  - ➤ The Reconstruction Finance Corporation lent money to businesses in trouble and made some small loans to farmers.
  - ➤ A huge road and dam building scheme created jobs.
  - ➤ He made $300 million available so states could help their unemployed – but only $30 million was actually accepted.
- Some of Hoover's actions made things worse. The Hawley-Smoot tariff (1930) taxed foreign goods, in the hope that Americans would buy the cheaper US goods. But other nations taxed incoming US goods, so US exports fell sharply, and even more businesses failed.

Violence and protest

- Farmers in Iowa used guns and pitchforks to chase away government officials who tried to evict farm owners.
- In the summer of 1932, 25,000 unemployed ex-soldiers marched to Washington DC and asked for their war pension (or 'bonus') to be paid early. Hoover set the army on them, who drove the 'Bonus Army' away with guns, tanks and tear-gas.

 APPLY

INTERPRETATION ANALYSIS

a Explain the following in no more than 15 words:
- Hooverville
- breadline
- hobo.

b Look at these interpretations about the Great Depression.

▼ **INTERPRETATION A** *Raymond Tarver, interviewed in 1940 for the Federal Writers' Project, a US government scheme; he was from a small town in south Georgia:*

I worked for the First National Bank. I was not wealthy at the time of the panic but I had some savings and a good job. That was the trouble – my savings and my job disappeared at the same time. Even so I was more concerned about our customers. The saddest part was to see the widows, who had probably just been left just a little insurance money and they put it in the bank. What were they going to live off now?

▼ **INTERPRETATION B** *Jerome Zerbe, interviewed for a book published in 1970; he was from a rich American family, who lived in Manhattan, one of New York's wealthiest areas, during the Depression; a Cadillac is an expensive car:*

One day I saw this pathetic beggar, whom I'd always felt sorry for. This Cadillac drove up. And I'd just given him a quarter. And it picked him up. There was a woman driving it. And I thought: well, if they can drive a Cadillac, they don't need my quarter. His wife had a Cadillac. And I never saw breadlines, never in New York. If they were, they were in Harlem. They were never in this section of town. There were never any signs of poverty. The thirties was a glamorous, glittering moment.

c 1 How does **Interpretation B** differ from **Interpretation A** about the impact of the Depression? Explain your answer using **Interpretations A** and **B**.

2 Why might the authors of **Interpretations A** and **B** have a different interpretation about the impact of the Depression? Explain your answer using **Interpretations A** and **B** and your contextual knowledge.

3 Which interpretation do you find more convincing about the impact of the Depression? Explain your answer using **Interpretations A** and **B** and your contextual knowledge.

IN WHAT WAYS

a Create a spider diagram showing 'The effects of the Depression on America'. Colour-code your diagram to highlight **economic effects**, **social effects**, and **both economic and social effects**.

b In what ways were American people affected by the Great Depression?

EXAMINER TIP

This question asks you to write about the *impact* the Depression had on US citizens – and explore how their lives changed.

The 1932 presidential election

The two main candidates for the 1932 presidential election were Herbert Hoover, who was hoping to be re-elected, and Franklin Delano Roosevelt (FDR).

 Herbert Hoover (1874–1964)

Background

- Orphaned aged eight, raised by two uncles.
- Made his fortune in the mining industry.
- Multi-millionaire by the age of 40.
- Retired from mining to enter politics.

Political party

- Republican Party.
- Believed it wasn't government's role to interfere in the daily lives of citizens ('laissez-faire').

Political career

- Excellent early career in politics, especially during the First World War.
- Elected president in 1928, during the economic boom.

Ideas for dealing with the Depression

- Thought of Americans as 'rugged individuals', able to overcome any problem without government help and achieve success through their own hard work (like him!).
- Only after a few years of Depression did he lend money to troubled businesses and farms, make cash available to states to help their unemployed and begin large-scale construction projects.
- Hoover was not a good public speaker and his belief in rugged individualism made him look uncaring, which made him unpopular.

REVIEW

To remind yourself of the measures Hoover took during the early years of the Depression, go to page 35.

 **Franklin Delano Roosevelt (1882–1945)**

Background

- Privately educated only child from a very rich family.

Political party

- Democratic Party
- His wife (Eleanor) may have influenced his decision to be a Democrat. Many of FDR's family were Republicans.

Political career

- Helped organise the navy during the First World War.
- Contracted polio, a spinal disease that nearly killed him, in 1921. Used a wheelchair for the rest of his life.
- Re-entered politics in 1928, becoming Governor of New York.

Ideas for dealing with the Depression

- As Governor of New York, spent $20 million of tax money helping the unemployed.
- If elected, he promised America the '3 Rs':
  - ➤ Relief: help for the old, sick, unemployed and homeless
  - ➤ Recovery: government schemes to provide jobs
  - ➤ Reform: to make America a better place for ordinary people and ensure another Depression could not happen.

Roosevelt's election as president

- FDR called his new ideas 'a New Deal for the American people'.
- An excellent public speaker, he took his message around the country, sometimes making 15 speeches a day.
- Some historians believe that voters liked him because he had succeeded despite his disability – they thought he had the right experience to help America recover.
- The phrase 'New Deal' caught the public's imagination and led FDR to one of the biggest election victories in US history.

SUMMARY

- In October 1929, Wall Street 'crashed' and millions of people lost money on the stock market.
- Many Americans had borrowed money from banks to buy shares, and when they couldn't pay it back, the banks went bankrupt.
- The Wall Street Crash led to the Great Depression, which had a major negative impact on the US economy and society.
- President Hoover, a Republican, attempted to deal with the effects of the Depression, but it was too little, too late.
- In 1932, a Democrat named Franklin Roosevelt became president and promised Americans a 'New Deal'.

APPLY

BULLET POINTS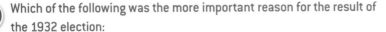

a Create 4 revision cards each for Hoover and Roosevelt. Use the following titles:

- Background
- Political party
- Political career
- Ideas for dealing with the Depression

b What impact do you think the following had on the presidential election:

- laissez-faire
- rugged individualism
- 'New deal'
- '3Rs'?

c **EXAM QUESTION** Which of the following was the more important reason for the result of the 1932 election:

- Hoover's belief in laissez-faire and rugged individualism
- FDR's 1932 political campaign?

Explain your answer with reference to both bullet points.

EXAMINER TIP

Make sure you explore both bullet points and examine their impact on the election.

CHAPTER 5

The effectiveness of the New Deal

 **RECAP**

The New Deal

In the first 100 days of FDR's presidency, Americans saw more action being taken to end the Depression than they had seen since it began. The 'laissez-faire' attitude of the previous presidency was over.

The Emergency Banking Act	The Economy Act	The Beer Act
Confidence in America's banking system was at an all-time low. FDR temporarily closed all banks and had them inspected. Only honest, well-run banks with enough cash would be given loans and reopened. When they did, people put money back into their accounts. Well-run banks could now lend money to well-run businesses, which would create jobs as businesses expanded.	All government employees' pay was cut by 15 per cent, saving nearly $1 billion.	Prohibition was ended, putting the gangsters out of business. The government could raise money by taxing alcohol.

REVIEW ↻

Remind yourself of the Republican policy of laissez-faire on page 12.

The Alphabet Agencies

FDR created new organisations to deal with some of the country's problems. They were nicknamed 'Alphabet Agencies' because they were known by their initials. FDR's theory behind this was simple:

The government creates jobs by spending money. → Once the workers earn wages, they start buying goods. ⇄ Firms and businesses then start hiring new workers.

Some people used the phrase 'priming the pump' to describe this idea.

FCA (Farm Credit Administration)

Lent money to farmers who couldn't keep up with loan payments.

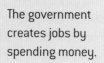
Help for farmers

AAA (Agricultural Adjustment Agency)

Paid farmers to produce less. As a result, food prices rose and farmers' incomes increased. However, the AAA was criticised because food was being destroyed while millions went hungry.

NRA (National Recovery Administration)

Encouraged workers and employers to work out a code of fair conditions and pay and gave workers the right to join a trade union. However, it was a voluntary scheme and many employers refused to join, leading to strikes.

Help for industry and workers

TVA (Tennessee Valley Authority)

Provided work building dams and electric power stations along the Tennessee River area, one of the poorest in America.

HOLC (Home Owners Loan Corporation)

Gave loans to people struggling to pay their mortgages.

CCC (Civilian Conservation Corps)
Jobless 18- to 25-year-olds were put to work in the countryside, creating 2.5 million jobs.

CWA (Civil Works Administration)
Provided temporary jobs for 4 million people, building schools, airports and roads.

Help for the unemployed

FERA (Federal Emergency Relief Agency)
$500 million was given to states to help the homeless. Soup kitchens, blankets, clothes and nursery school places were provided.

Opposition to the New Deal

Not everyone liked FDR's New Deal. Some thought it interfered too much in ordinary Americans' lives, while others believed it didn't help people enough.

The rich
To pay for the New Deal, FDR raised taxes for rich people, which angered them.

Business people
Many business owners didn't like the way the New Deal agencies 'interfered' with business and gave more rights to workers.

The Supreme Court
America's highest court, the Supreme Court, ruled that the AAA Alphabet Agency was illegal. It said that giving help to farmers was a matter for state governments, not the federal government. The Supreme Court also declared many of the NRA codes illegal.

Republicans
Many Republicans who believed in ideas like 'laissez-faire' and 'rugged individualism' were horrified by the way the New Deal dominated people's lives. Some said Roosevelt was behaving like a dictator and making the government too powerful.

Radical politicians' ideas for an alternative New Deal

- Huey Long: Louisiana politician. Suggested an alternative for the New Deal called 'Share Our Wealth': all fortunes over $5 million would be confiscated and shared out and every family would receive $5000 to buy a radio, a car and a house. He also promised cheap food for the poor, houses for war veterans and free education. His ideas were **radical**, but he was popular.
- Francis Townsend: retired doctor from California. Wanted everyone to retire at 60 to give more job opportunities to younger people.
- Charles Coughlin: Set up the 'National Union for Social Justice', which aimed to provide work and fair wages for everyone. However, he made speeches attacking Jewish people and trade unions, and his support declined.

APPLY

DESCRIBE

a   Choose six of FDR's laws, ideas, schemes or agencies and complete a chart like this. An example has been done for you.

Action by FDR	Brief explanation	How it helped the country	Criticisms/issues
The Beer Act	Ended Prohibition	Gangsters were put out of business; government could raise money by taxing alcohol, which could be spent on government schemes.	The people who were in favour of Prohibition would have been disappointed.

b   Explain why each of the following opposed FDR's New Deal:

- The rich
- The Supreme Court
- Business people
- Republicans.

c   **EXAM QUESTION** Describe two criticisms of the New Deal.
[Taken from AQA 2016 Paper 1 specimen material]

EXAMINER TIP
Do not spend any time describing the New Deal – just write about *two* ways in which it was criticised.

The effectiveness of the New Deal

Some people say that while the New Deal created lots of jobs, it failed to solve unemployment completely. Some critics argued that the New Deal 'interfered' too much in citizens' lives and wasted money on work programmes.

Defenders of FDR point out that the New Deal helped groups in society that had previously been neglected by the government – farmers and the very poor, for example. One of FDR's proudest achievements was the Social Security Act (SSA) of 1935, America's first system of social welfare. It included a national system of pensions for the elderly, widows and disabled people and payments for the sick and unemployed.

- The New Deal created jobs. For example, 2.5 million 18-to 25-year-olds got work in the CCC. However, at least one in ten people was unemployed in the USA throughout the 1930s.
- The number of bank failures dropped dramatically during the New Deal era.
- The number of days workers went on strike increased in 1934. However, by 1938 it had dropped to 1932 levels.
- Gross National Product (GNP) rose steadily from 1933 to 1941.

However, millions remained very poor throughout the 1930s.

The New Deal and workers

- The Alphabet Agencies provided work for many skilled and unskilled workers.
- When the Supreme Court declared the NRA's fair labour and wages codes illegal, FDR introduced the Wagner Act. This gave workers the right to join a trade union.
- However, unions were treated with suspicion by some employers.

The New Deal and farmers

- Measures were introduced to help raise the price of crops and make loans available to farmers to save them from eviction. Most help went to large-scale farmers; small-scale farmers and farm workers did not see much benefit.
- There was still severe poverty in much of rural America.

The New Deal and African-Americans

- The New Deal did not seek to end the severe discrimination – for example, CCC campsites were segregated.
- However, 200,000 African-Americans gained jobs in the CCC, and one African-American woman, Mary McLeod Bethune, was appointed to an important government post.

The New Deal and women

- There were no New Deal programmes aimed directly at women, but many found work with one of the Alphabet Agencies or were helped by the SSA.
- However, women still faced discrimination. For example, some of the NRA codes set women's wages lower than men's.

The New Deal and American Indians

- Government loans were provided for American Indians to buy more land, set up businesses and buy farming equipment.
- The Indian Reservation Act of 1934 gave American Indians the right to manage their own affairs.
- However, many still lived in great poverty and suffered discrimination.

 APPLY

IN WHAT WAYS

a Explain whether you think each of the following people did well or badly out of the New Deal. Would they be happy, angry, or perhaps both?

- A farmer's wife in the Tennessee Valley
- Henry Ford
- A Ford car worker
- An African-American restaurant worker
- A small-scale farmer in the Dust Bowl.

b FDR stated that the New Deal should provide relief, recovery and reform. To what extent did the New Deal achieve its aims?

c
> **EXAM QUESTION** In what ways did the US economy change as a result of FDR's New Deal?

EXAMINER TIP

Make sure you focus on the changes that took place relating to the US economy, rather than how lives changed or didn't change for certain groups of people.

REVIEW

Look back at page 37 to remind yourself of the '3 Rs'. This was what FDR promised the American people.

INTERPRETATION ANALYSIS

a Look at these interpretations about the New Deal.

▼ **INTERPRETATION A** *A trained designer interviewed in 1939 for the Federal Writers' Project, a US government scheme. He lost his job at the start of the Great Depression but got work with one of the Alphabet Agencies (the Works Progress Administration – WPA) in Newburyport, Massachusetts:*

> All I can say is from where I'm standing, things are better now. I'm not work shy, I'm not a bum – I'm just a guy who needed a break. All the President's trying to do is pull the United States out of a rut. I mean, you can't blame the man for trying, can you?

▼ **INTERPRETATION B** *A man from a wealthy American family, who lived in Manhattan, one of New York's wealthiest areas, during the Depression. He is speaking in the 1960s in response to the question 'What does the phrase "New Deal" mean to you?':*

> It meant absolutely nothing except higher taxation. And that he did. He obviously didn't help the poverty situation in this country, although, I suppose. I don't know.

EXAMINER TIP

Remember to write about both interpretations, making reference to your contextual knowledge. You could look at pages 7 and 8 for advice on how to respond to these types of questions.

b
> **EXAM QUESTION**
> 1 How does **Interpretation B** differ from **Interpretation A** about FDR's New Deal? Explain your answer using **Interpretations A** and **B**.
>
> 2 Why might the authors of **Interpretations A** and **B** have a different interpretation about FDR's New Deal?
>
> 3 Which interpretation do you find more convincing about FDR's New Deal? Explain your answer using **Interpretations A** and **B** and your contextual knowledge.

RECAP

The end of the New Deal

When FDR was re-elected in November 1936, he was increasingly worried by the cost of his job creation schemes.

- He cut the amount spent on New Deal programmes – but unemployment jumped by 3 million because the government was no longer creating so many jobs.

- Thousands of workers in the car and steel industries went on strike as part of the campaign for better wages and conditions.

- Unemployment rose to 10.5 million in 1938, and car and steel production kept falling.

- By January 1939, FDR himself acknowledged that the New Deal had come to an end.

Popular culture in 1930s America

The term 'popular culture' refers to the common ideas, customs and behaviour of a particular group or country at a particular time in history. This could be the music they listened to, the films or television shows people watched, and the books they read.

Music

- Jazz remained popular, and jazz artists such as Louis Armstrong, Duke Ellington and Billie Holiday sold huge numbers of records.
- Performers such as Glenn Miller, Judy Garland and Bing Crosby also found fame.
- Most people listened to music through the radio, but gramophone sales increased as vinyl records became more widely available.
- Radios broadcast poetry, plays, news reports, live sport and variety shows.

Cinema

- One of the most popular leisure activities of the 1930s – over 100 million people went to the cinema each week.
- Musicals (such as *42nd Street*), comedies starring Charlie Chaplin and Laurel and Hardy, Walt Disney cartoons, historical dramas (such as *Gone with the Wind*) and horror films (such as *Frankenstein* and *Dracula*) were incredibly popular.

Comic books

- First appeared in the early 1930s, but their popularity soared after the publication of *Action Comics* (1938), which included the debut of Superman.
- Comics were bright, cheap, easy to read and provided an escape into a world of adventure.

Literature

- Authors such as Erskine Caldwell, John Steinbeck and James T Farrell wrote about the Great Depression and the poverty, racism and social problems they witnessed.

The arts

- The Works Progress Administration (WPA) was one of FDR's Alphabet Agencies that provided work for unemployed artists of all kinds.
  - Actors were hired to put on free shows.
  - Artists painted pictures for display in schools, libraries and parks.
  - Writers produced guidebooks on every US state.
- Much of this artistic output still exists today – and it made many Americans more aware of their own traditions, history and culture.
- The WPA was criticised for wasting taxpayers' money.

Timeline

1932	First Mickey Mouse colour cartoon
1933	Prohibition ends
1934	Masters golf tournament is held for first time
1935	Rumba dance becomes popular; Monopoly goes on sale
1936	Bass guitar is invented
1937	Disney's *Snow White and the Seven Dwarfs* is released
1938	Chocolate chip cookie is developed

SUMMARY

- FDR introduced many new laws, schemes, organisations and agencies to try to deal with the problems caused by the Great Depression.

- FDR's ideas became known as the 'New Deal'.

- The impact of the New Deal was mixed. Some of the reforms made a positive impact, while others did not have the impact that was hoped for.

- Popular culture in the 1930s retained some influences from the 1920s (such as jazz music and the cinema), but there were also new influences such as comic books and literature inspired by the Great Depression.

APPLY

DESCRIBE

a Define the term 'popular culture' in no more than 20 words.

b Make a set of revision cards for each of the types of popular culture on these pages. Jot down three or four points on each card. Try to include specific factual details, for example names, dates, named examples, etc.

c **EXAM QUESTION** Describe two developments in popular culture in the 1930s.

EXAMINER TIP

In 'describe' questions, you do not have to explain why you have chosen the two ways – just describe them.

IN WHAT WAYS

a Give two examples of how popular culture in the 1930s had changed from the 1920s.

b Give two examples of similarities.

INTERPRETATION ANALYSIS

a Look at this interpretation about movies in the 1930s.

▼ **INTERPRETATION A** *From Alice Fairweather, a poor farmer's wife from the Southern states of America, interviewed in 1939 for the Federal Writers' Project, a US government scheme; 'picture show' refers to a film shown in a cinema:*

> I don't believe in dancing. And our preacher, he don't think the picture shows is right, neither. I guess the children might like the shows, but I wouldn't want them to go, even if we had plenty of money, for they'd just learn mischief.

b Sum up what Alice Fairweather says about the movies.

c Can you suggest reasons why she might feel this way?

REVISION SKILLS

Draw – use sketches, doodles and pictures to help make facts memorable. You do not have to be a good artist to do this!

CHAPTER 6

The impact of the Second World War

From isolationism to world war

- America followed a policy of **isolationism** after the First World War, keeping out of the affairs of other countries. Instead, the USA concentrated on building up its economy and strong trade links.
- In October 1937, FDR said peace-loving nations should break off relations with aggressive nations. It was clear that he was referring to Germany, Italy and Japan, which had been taking over other nations in Europe, Africa and the Far East.
- When war began in Europe in September 1939, America declared support for Britain and France against Germany and its allies. FDR was also concerned about Japan's aggressiveness in the Far East, where America did much trade and controlled large areas of land.
- In November 1939, the USA began to help Britain and France against Germany:
  - ➤ The Cash and Carry Plan – America sold Britain and France US weapons, which created valuable production jobs at a time of rising unemployment.
  - ➤ **Lend Lease**: from March 1941, America started to 'lend' weapons to Britain. The USA struck a similar deal with the USSR when Germany attacked it in June 1941.

> **REVIEW** ↻
>
> Go to page 14 to remind yourself of America's role and economic position at the end of the First World War.

Reaction in America

Officially, America was a neutral country, but it was clear that the US government supported Britain's war against Germany. This caused mixed reactions in the USA:

- Organisations such as the Mothers' Crusade and the America First Committee held big anti-war demonstrations.
- Others saw the economic benefits. As America began to rearm in case it was forced to enter the war, millions found jobs building fighter planes, battleships and tanks, or in the armed forces.

Japan and Pearl Harbor

- During the 1930s, Japan began to invade many of the surrounding countries, seizing food and raw materials.
- In protest at Japan's aggression, FDR vowed not to sell any oil or steel to Japan, which angered the Japanese.
- On Sunday 7 December 1941, Japanese bomber planes attacked Pearl Harbor, an American naval base in Hawaii. Twenty-one US warships were sunk or damaged, 177 US planes were destroyed and over 2000 men were killed.
- The next day, America and Britain declared war on Japan. Three days later, Germany and Italy, Japan's allies, declared war on America.

Weapon making

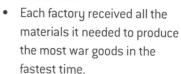

- The War Production Board (WPB) was created to convert industries from peacetime work to war work.
- Each factory received all the materials it needed to produce the most war goods in the fastest time.
- In 1943, US factories produced 86,000 planes – and 96,000 in 1944 (28,000 more than Germany and Japan combined).

America at war

Unemployment

- Unemployment dropped as America began to rearm.
- By 1941, around 4 million people had found jobs in the armed forces or building fighter planes, battleships and tanks. Between 1939 and 1944, unemployment dropped from 9.5 million to just 670,000.
- Farmers prospered because they supplied food to the military.
- The traditional industries of coal, iron, steel and oil were all boosted by the demands of war.

Women

- Before the war, women had worked in traditional 'female' jobs such as nursing or teaching.
- As millions of men joined up, women began to fill their places in factories, railways and shipyards. Around 350,000 women joined women's sections of the armed forces.
- Between 1940 and 1945, the number of women in work rose from 12 million to nearly 19 million. Women now occupied a third of all America's jobs.

African-Americans

- In June 1941, the government set up the Fair Employment Practice Committee (FEPC) to help prevent discrimination against African-Americans in defence and government jobs.
- The FEPC could not force companies to change, but it could recommend that they didn't receive profitable government contracts. As a result, some companies improved their policies in relation to African-American workers.
- Around a million African-Americans fought in the war, but there was still widespread discrimination in the armed services. For example:
  - ➤ Black sailors were only allowed to work in ships' kitchens.
  - ➤ Black soldiers were not allowed to train as officers.
  - ➤ Initially, the air force wouldn't train black pilots.
- However, as the war went on, the racial barriers began to break down:
  - ➤ The air force allowed African-Americans to train as pilots (although they had to fight in 'blacks only' squadrons).
  - ➤ All of the armed services trained black officers (but they could only lead other black soldiers in segregated units).
  - ➤ African-American women were also permitted to become nurses, but they were only allowed to treat black soldiers.

SUMMARY

- America's policy of isolationism ended in the late 1930s; America supplied weapons to Britain, France and the USSR.
- After the Japanese attack on Pearl Harbor in 1941, the USA declared war on Japan and Germany.
- Service in the armed forces and weapons production helped the US economy.
- The war changed the lives of women and African-Americans.

 APPLY

BULLET POINTS

a Explain the following terms in no more than 15 words:
- isolationism
- Cash and Carry Plan
- Lend Lease.

b What did the WPB do?

c Copy and complete the chart below:

Group in US society	Before the war	Impact of the war on the group
Unemployed		
Women		
African-Americans		

d

 EXAM QUESTION Which of the following groups experienced more change during the Second World War:
- the unemployed and women
- African-Americans?

EXAMINER TIP

Make sure you write about each of the groups affected, but come to a final decision on which group was affected most. It is important you focus on the impact of war on the economy here, not on the social impact on women or African-Americans.

Post-war American society and economy

 **RECAP**

The 'American Dream'

After the Second World War, peacetime goods were produced in the same, efficient way that war goods were. Post-war America saw an era of **consumerism** – the concept that the ever-expanding consumption of goods benefits the economy. Millions of Americans might have said that they were 'living the American Dream' at this time – the idea that anyone could succeed through hard work.

Luxury goods, such as refrigerators, ovens, vacuum cleaners, cars and televisions were produced at affordable prices. Demand was high because these goods were rare during the war.

By the end of the 1950s, nine out of every ten US households had a television, eight had a car and a telephone and seven had a washing machine.

A powerful advertising industry and 'buy now, pay later' schemes persuaded people to spend money.

Consumer society in post-war America

There was a boom in overseas spending on US-made goods. By 1952, America was supplying the world with 65 per cent of its manufactured goods.

Huge shopping centres (malls) that sold all sorts of goods were built on the outskirts of large towns and cities. Some city centres declined as people went 'out-of-town' to shop.

America experienced a 'baby boom' that saw a 40 per cent increase in the population.

Truman's 'Fair Deal'

After his death in April 1945 FDR was replaced by Harry S Truman. Like FDR, Truman felt it was important for the government to help bring about a fairer society. Truman called his plans the 'Fair Deal'. The two main issues he hoped to tackle were poverty and the rights of African-Americans.

- ✓ Truman raised the minimum hourly wage from 40 cents to 75 cents.
- ✓ Large areas of slum housing were cleared to make way for affordable homes.
- ✓ The GI Bill made cheap home loans available to war veterans and grants were paid for ex-soldiers to attend college or trade schools. From 1944 to 1949, the government gave around $4 billion to nearly 9 million veterans.
- ✗ Truman's proposal to introduce a national health insurance scheme was blocked by Republicans.
- ✗ An attempt to improve the rights of African-Americans was halted when many Southern politicians voted against it.

Women after the war

- After doing such valuable war work, most women went back to their more traditional roles as housewives.
- Women who did get jobs were often employed in traditionally 'female' roles – nursing, teaching and secretarial work.

- Women who tried to pursue a high-flying business or management career often faced discrimination. As a result, a growing number of women in the late 1950s – particularly middle-class women – became increasingly frustrated.
- By 1950, the average age at which a woman got married was 20 – the lowest since 1890. There was a (mostly male) view that 'a woman's place was in the home' – and that she was 'living the American Dream' if she had all the latest gadgets.

A new president

In 1952, Republican Dwight 'Ike' Eisenhower became president. He brought lots of business people into the government to keep the economy booming. But despite improvements in living standards and rising wages:

- There were still vast areas (mainly in the South) where most people were desperately poor with sub-standard housing and schools.
- There was no national health service that guaranteed a basic level of healthcare for everyone, or jobseekers' or sickness pay.
- The elderly failed to benefit from the boom. In 1960, 68 per cent of people over 65 had an annual income of less than $1000, while average factory earnings were over $4000.

The Rock and Roll generation

As America grew wealthier, teenagers had more leisure time and spending power than in previous generations.

- The booming economy meant many parents could help their children financially. One of the key ideas of the 'American Dream' was that each generation is more successful than the previous one.
- Children no longer had to get a job to support the family when they reached 14 or 15, so many children finished high school and went to college.
- In 1957, the average teenager spent between $10 and $15 a week (compared to $1–$2 in the early 1940s).
- Teenagers often spent their money on music, cars, fashion and alcohol. Some teenage boys raced cars and formed gangs.
- Teenagers soon got a reputation for being independent, rebellious, secretive and aggressive. Figures like James Dean and Marlon Brando became emblems of teenage rebellion.
- A new style of music called 'Rock and Roll' was very popular among teenagers.
- Before long, Rock and Roll was viewed by many as 'dangerous' and was linked to teenage crime and gang culture.
- By the end of the 1950s, nine out of every ten US households had a television. Televised Rock and Roll made TV extremely popular with teenagers. A 1956 TV performance by Elvis Presley was watched by 82 per cent of Americans.

APPLY

IN WHAT WAYS

a Define the following terms in no more than 20 words:
- consumerism • Fair Deal • Rock and Roll generation.

b Make a list of ways in which life in 1950s America was different from life during the war, or during the 1930s.

c  **In what ways did the prosperity of American citizens show itself in the 1950s?**

EXAMINER TIP

For this question, you might write that many consumer goods were rare during the war, or that people couldn't afford them during the Depression of the 1930s – but by the 1950s they were cheaper and readily available again.

EXAMINER TIP

This question does not simply want you to write about life in the 1950s, it wants you to think about how life had changed. Remember – it's important to think about whether life changed for *everyone*.

 **RECAP**

The growing fear of communism

Many Americans had a deep-seated fear of communism. A second 'Red Scare' took place in the years immediately after the Second World War, up until the mid-1950s.

The Soviet Union had developed nuclear weapons, just like the USA. They were rival **superpowers** with very different political systems (communism in the Soviet Union and capitalism in America). There was concern that the rivalry could develop into a devastating nuclear war. This period of rivalry between the countries was known as the Cold War.

Communists were often known as 'Reds'. To refresh your memory of the first 'Red Scare' of the 1920s, see pages 30 and 31.

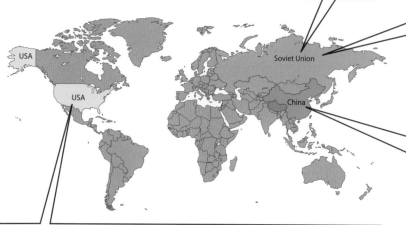

Many countries in eastern Europe were under the communist influence of the Soviet Union. Americans worried that communism might spread to the USA.

The US government vowed to stop the spread of communism using a policy called '**containment**'. In the late 1940s, China (another huge nation with vast reserves of raw materials) became a communist state. This increased fear that containment wasn't working, and communism was spreading.

A member of the US government (Alger Hiss) was accused of spying for the Soviet Union. Americans Ethel and Julius Rosenberg were found guilty of spying and executed in June 1953. These scandals became headline news, and the fear that there were communists at work across America grew.

'Un-American activities'

- A US government group (the **HUAC** or **H**ouse of Representatives **U**n-American **A**ctivities **C**ommittee) began searching for communists in the US government, in workplaces, in the media and in the movie industry.
- President Truman introduced a Loyalty Programme that allowed the Federal Bureau of Investigation (FBI) to investigate all government employees and sack any 'security risks'.
- Millions of Americans were investigated by the HUAC and the Loyalty Programmes between 1947 and 1950. Although none were found guilty of spying, many were forced out of their jobs because of the 'disgrace' associated with their investigation.

McCarthyism

In 1950, politician Joseph McCarthy used the fear of communism to help further his political career by claiming he had a list of over 200 communists working for the government.

This caused a sensation and McCarthy's list was front page news. Many saw anti-communist McCarthy as a hero.

People who criticised him were accused of being supporters of communism, which could get them sacked.

For the next five years, McCarthy waged a wild campaign of investigations. Some likened it to a 'witch hunt'.

In 1954, McCarthy accused 45 army officers of being communist, but he had no evidence and '**McCarthyism**' began to lose public support.

SUMMARY

- America's post-war economy boomed, but millions of Americans still lived in desperate poverty.

- After the war, most women went back to their more traditional roles as housewives.

- A new 'Rock and Roll generation' of teenagers emerged in the 1950s.

- A deep-seated fear of communism returned in the 1950s as a second 'Red Scare' took place.

- Senator Joseph McCarthy gained national fame after accusing hundreds of people of being communists.

 **APPLY**

BULLET POINTS

a Create a 10-question quiz to test detailed knowledge about McCarthyism and the impact it had on post-war American society. You could swap the test with a friend.

b
> **EXAM QUESTION** Which of the following had more impact on people in post-war America:
> - McCarthyism
> - changes in the US economy?

EXAMINER TIP

You will need to look at pages 46–47, as well as these pages, to answer this question fully.

REVISION SKILLS

Repetition is vital for good long-term memory. Plan revision sessions in short bursts of 20–30 minutes several times a day.

INTERPRETATION ANALYSIS

a Look at this interpretation about McCarthyism.

▼ **INTERPRETATION A** *From an interview with Lee Grant on the 1999 US TV series* The Century: America's Time. *Grant is an American actress and film director who was nominated for an Oscar in 1951. In 1952, she refused to testify against her husband at the HUAC hearings and was 'blacklisted' from most acting jobs for the next ten years. It also contributed to her divorce. When she speaks of informers, she is talking about the people in the film industry who accused others of 'un-American activities'.*

> It was scary. It was very, very scary. Being an informer and placing your fellow actor or fellow friend, fellow director in jeopardy meant that that family didn't work anymore. So that taking that step was about the worst thing that you could do to anybody.
>
> © ABC News

b What impact could an accusation of 'un-American activities' have on a person's career and family?

c What happened to Grant during the period of McCarthyism?

d What do you think Grant thinks about this era in US history? Suggest reasons why she feels this way.

CHAPTER 8

Racial tension and developments in the civil rights campaigns

 **RECAP**

The Civil Rights Movement

- 'Civil rights' refers to equal opportunities with regards to access to employment, housing and education, as well as the right to vote and be free of racial discrimination.
- The **Civil Rights Movement** was a campaign that took place from the 1940s to the late 1960s.
- The aim was to achieve civil rights for African-Americans equal to those of white Americans.
- The Civil Rights Movement had already had some small success in the 1940s such as the 'Fair Employment Law' in 1941 and Truman's 1946 President's Committee on Civil Rights to try to eliminate segregation in American life.

> **REVIEW**
>
> Remind yourself of the Jim Crow Laws and segregation by looking back to pages 28–29.

Early successes of the Civil Rights Movement

'Brown v Board of Education of Topeka, 1954'

- Most of America's schools were segregated. In 1951, in Topeka, Kansas, the father of an African-American girl named Linda Brown took the local education authority (the Board of Education) to court. He wanted his daughter to attend her local 'whites only' school.
- He was helped in his case by the NAACP (National Association for the Advancement of Colored People).
- Brown lost the case but appealed against the decision to the Supreme Court.
- In May 1954, the Chief Judge declared that every education board had to end segregation in schools.
- Within weeks, many cities and towns began to 'de-segregate' their schools.

- However, some states refused to de-segregate. In the Southern state of Mississippi, a White Citizens Council was formed to ensure segregation would remain.
- By 1956, not a single African-American child was attending any school where there were white students in six Southern states.

The Montgomery Bus Boycott

- In Montgomery, Alabama, like in many Southern states, the buses were segregated. On 1 December 1955, Rosa Parks, an African-American woman, refused to move from the 'whites only' section. She was arrested.
- Rosa Parks was the secretary of the local NAACP and news of her arrest spread fast. Local black community leaders agreed to call a boycott of all city buses. Church preacher Martin Luther King led the boycott.
- The boycott lasted many months. African-Americans had provided 75 per cent of the bus company's business, which was soon in financial difficulty.
- Some of the protesters begin to receive threatening phone calls and their homes were vandalised – but King told the black community to remain peaceful. He believed that non-violent protest, or 'direct action', was the best way to achieve equal rights.
- Almost a year after Parks refused to give up her seat, the Supreme Court ruled that segregated buses, like schools, were illegal. This was a significant victory for the Civil Rights Movement and for peaceful direct action.

The importance of the Little Rock case

- In September 1957, nine African-American pupils tried to attend Central High School in Little Rock, Arkansas.

- Arkansas had refused to de-segregate its schools and Central High remained a school for white children.

- The governor of Arkansas sent National Guard soldiers to prevent the black children from entering the school. A large, hostile crowd greeted the children.

- The African-Americans of Little Rock took the governor to court – and won. The soldiers were forced to leave, and the pupils now had the right to go to the school.

- However, by 1960, out of Arkansas' 2 million black students, only 2500 were going to the same school as white children.

- By 1962, there were still no black children attending white schools in Alabama, South Carolina or Mississippi.

APPLY

DESCRIBE

a Define the term 'Civil Rights Movement' in no more than 20 words.

b Complete the following chart:

Event	Date	Brief description	Impact on Civil Rights Movement
President's Committee on Civil Rights			
'Brown v Board of Education of Topeka'			
Montgomery Bus Boycott			
The Little Rock case			

c **EXAM QUESTION** Describe two successes of the Civil Rights Movement.

EXAMINER TIP

Start your second 'success' on a new line, so that the examiner can easily see that you are providing what the question asks for.

A new Civil Rights law

- In 1957, a Civil Rights Act was passed giving all African-Americans the right to vote, but little was done to enforce it.
- However, it showed that the government was no longer willing to accept that the states could ignore federal government when it came to the rights of African-Americans.

Developments in the Civil Rights Movement

Protest

When: May 1963 (Alabama), August 1963 (Washington DC) and March 1965 (Selma).

Who: Martin Luther King and thousands of civil rights protesters.

What:

Alabama

- King organised a non-violent protest march in one of the most segregated cities in the USA – Birmingham, Alabama.
- The police, under the orders of the police chief, Eugene 'Bull' Connor, attacked the protesters with dogs, water cannons, tear-gas, electric cattle prods and batons.
- The arrest of hundreds of protesters, including 900 children, was shown on TV.
- President Kennedy sent in troops to restore order. He ordered Birmingham city council to end segregation.

Washington DC

- King spoke at the largest civil rights demonstration in US history and gave his most famous speech, known as 'I have a dream'.

Selma

- King organised another march from Selma to Birmingham, Alabama.
- When the marchers reached the outskirts of Selma they were brutally attacked by local police.
- The day became known as 'Bloody Sunday'.

Sit-ins and freedom rides

When: Early 1960s.

Who: Martin Luther King, black and white civil rights 'Freedom Riders' and campaigners.

What:

- African-American and white civil rights campaigners travelled sitting next to each other in 'whites only' sections of buses in areas where the local authorities had refused to de-segregate the buses. They were called 'Freedom Riders'.
- African-American students, sometimes accompanied by white students, would take a seat in the 'whites only' part of a café or restaurant and refuse to leave. In 1960 and 1961, around 70,000 campaigners had staged 'sit-in' protests across the South.

The work of the US government

When: 1961–68

Who: Presidents Kennedy and Johnson

What:

- Just before his assassination in 1963, Kennedy had supported a new Civil Rights Act that aimed to give African-Americans full equality in housing and education.
- Kennedy's successor, Lyndon Johnson, introduced another Civil Rights Act in 1964 that outlawed racial discrimination in employment and segregation in public places.
- In 1965, the Voting Rights Act gave all Americans the right to vote (only passed into law by Congress in 1968).
- Interracial marriages were legalised in 1967.
- The 1968 Fair Housing Act made racial discrimination illegal when buying and renting houses and other property.

Malcolm X and the Black Power Movement

Some civil rights campaigners rejected the approach of people like Martin Luther King. They felt that change was not happening quickly enough; millions of African-Americans still faced poverty and poor education. Several organisations promoting 'black power' grew in the 1960s.

Extreme militant group that rejected King's non-violent ideas.

Around 5000 members by 1968.

The Black Panther Party

Argued that African-Americans needed to protect themselves from white racists, using violence if necessary.

Wanted separatism (keeping the races apart).

Said that white society was racist and corrupt.

Rejected Christianity as a white man's religion, urging African-Americans to follow Islam.

The Nation of Islam (also known as the Black Muslims)

The best-known member was Malcolm X. However, he later became less extreme in his views, left the Nation of Islam and set up the Organization of Afro-American Unity (OAAU) in 1964. While speaking at an OAAU meeting in 1965 he was shot and killed by Nation of Islam members.

SUMMARY

- The Civil Rights Movement had some notable successes in the 1950s with the 'Brown v Board of Education of Topeka, 1954' case, the Montgomery Bus Boycott of 1955 and the Little Rock case of 1957.

- Common forms of protest included marches, 'sit-ins' and freedom rides.

- Martin Luther King, Rosa Parks and Malcolm X are key African-American figures in the Civil Rights Movement.

- Some civil rights groups, such as the Black Panther Party, rejected King's peaceful methods.

- Significant Civil Rights Acts occurred in 1957, 1964 and 1968.

 APPLY

IN WHAT WAYS

a Create a spider diagram that outlines and assesses the Civil Rights Movement.

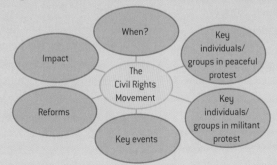

b EXAM QUESTION In what ways did Americans try to improve the civil rights of African-Americans?

 EXAMINER TIP

This question asks you to focus on the ways that Americans tried to change the civil rights of African-Americans. Remember that this refers to the way in which *all* Americans tried to change things – it might be the work of government as well as ordinary protesters.

America and the 'Great Society'

CHAPTER 9

President Kennedy's 'New Frontier'

During the presidencies of John F Kennedy (JFK) and Lyndon B Johnson (LBJ), a series of domestic programmes tried to eliminate poverty and inequality, improve education and fight unemployment. The series of reforms introduced by JFK was called the 'New Frontier'.

John F Kennedy's New Frontier

The economy

- JFK cut taxes to give people more money to spend.
- Made $900 million available to businesses to create new jobs.
- Gave grants to companies to buy high-tech equipment and train their workers to use it.
- Increased government spending on the armed forces, creating jobs.

Healthcare and poverty

- Minimum hourly wage increased.
- $4.9 billion made available for loans to improve housing, clear slum areas and build roads and telephone lines.
- Training schemes for the unemployed introduced.
- Social Security Act increased benefits for the elderly and unemployed.
- Increased funding for research into mental illness and allocated funds to develop poor rural areas.

Education

- The Peace Corps was set up – an organisation that sends volunteers abroad to assist people in poorer countries (it still exists today).

Criticisms of the New Frontier

- New equipment in factories sometimes meant that fewer workers were needed, so some people lost their jobs. Many new jobs were dependent on government spending, so were vulnerable to spending cuts.
- By 1963, unemployment stood at 4.5 million – only 1 million less than in 1960.
- The minimum wage was only helpful to those in work – and housing loans were only useful if the recipient could afford the loan repayments.
- JFK's efforts to provide funding for schools failed. Politicians from the Southern states (who had clashed with him over civil rights issues) refused to support his plans.
- The Commission on Equal Employment Opportunity (CEEO) helped those who already had a government job but did nothing to find jobs for millions of unemployed African-Americans. The black unemployment rate was twice that of white Americans.

REVIEW

Remind yourself of the other great domestic reform programme during the period of this book by looking at FDR's New Deal reforms on pages 38–42.

President Johnson's 'Great Society'

LBJ succeeded JFK as president after Kennedy's assassination. They were both Democrats.
LBJ's reform programmes were called the '**Great Society**'.

Lyndon B Johnson's Great Society

The economy

- The Job Corps was introduced to help high school leavers get jobs.
- The minimum hourly wage increased from $1.25 to $1.40.

Healthcare and poverty

- A Housing Act funded low-income housing.
- The Model Cities Act cleared up inner-city slums.
- Air and Water Quality Acts tightened controls over pollution.
- Safety standards were improved for consumer products.
- 'Medicare' was created (a JFK idea) to fund healthcare for the elderly and low income families.

Education

- 'Operation Headstart' gave money to poor schools in cities.
- The Elementary and Secondary Education Act provided major funding for schools.
- The Volunteers In Service To America (VISTA) programme was set up as a domestic version of the Peace Corps.
- The National Endowment for the Arts and Humanities gave grants to fund artists and galleries.

Criticisms of the Great Society

- Opinions on the Great Society vary dramatically. Supporters say that in 1959, for example, 56 per cent of African-Americans lived in desperate poverty, but by 1970 this had fallen to around 30 per cent; white families saw a reduction from 18 per cent to just 8 per cent.
- Despite this, many say LBJ spent far too much on his reforms. By 1968, unemployment was rising and there was widespread rioting in poorer areas of some cities.
- LBJ fully supported US involvement in the Vietnam War, which was becoming increasingly unpopular and costly.

 **APPLY**

IN WHAT WAYS

a Define 'New Frontier' and 'Great Society', using no more than 20 works for each.

b Make a set of revision cards for the domestic programmes of JFK and LBJ.

c **EXAM QUESTION** In what ways did LBJ try to fulfil his promise of a 'Great Society'?

REVISION SKILLS

Revision cards are a good way of revising and creating a useful revision aid for later use. Jot down three or four things under a heading on each card. Try to include a factual detail with each point.

EXAMINER TIP

Try to include something that was sucessful and something that was less successful from LBJ's programme.

The fight for equality

President Kennedy set up the Status Commission to report on women in the workplace:

Women earned around 60 per cent less than men.	**Report on women in the workplace, 1963**	Women could legally be dismissed if they married.
95 per cent of managers were male.	Most work for women was part-time, with limited responsibility.	Only 4 per cent of lawyers and 7 per cent of doctors were women.

In 1963, a best-selling book called *The Feminine Mystique* by Betty Friedan was published. It argued that well-qualified women felt depressed and undervalued because they were unable to pursue a fulfilling career. It called for equality between men and women.

In June 1963, Congress passed the Equal Pay Act, making it law that women and men receive equal pay for the same job. The 1964 Civil Rights Act banned discrimination based on race and sex in employment.

Feminist groups

Many felt that there was still widespread discrimination against women and Betty Friedan and others established the National Organization for Women (NOW) in 1966.

> **NOW** demanded complete equal rights for women in US law. Abortion was illegal in all US states. NOW stated it was a woman's right to make her own reproductive decisions.
>
> Within a few years NOW had around 40,000 members, mainly middle-aged and middle-class. They wrote to politicians, organised large demonstrations and took to court companies that failed to pay women the same wages as men.

Groups of younger, more extreme women used different approaches to highlight their cause, such as disrupting the 1968 Miss World Beauty Contest. They became known as the Women's Liberation Movement or 'Women's Lib'.

Other women's groups included the Women's Campaign Fund, the North American Indian Women's Association and the National Black Feminist Organization.

Collectively, these groups were known as the '**feminist movement**'.

Timeline Women's rights and the law

1965 All married couples allowed to use contraceptives

1969 California becomes first state to adopt a 'no fault' divorce law, allowing couples to divorce by 'mutual consent'

1972 Educational Amendment Act bans sexual discrimination in education – girls can study same subjects as boys

Equal Rights Amendment (ERA) and 'Stop ERA'

- Despite changes to the law, women's average pay remained well below men's and sex discrimination was still common.
- In 1972, the 'Equal Rights Amendment' (ERA) was approved by Congress. It stated that 'Equality of rights under the law shall not be denied by the United States or by any State on account of sex.'
- A 'Stop ERA' campaign, led by Phyllis Schlafly, opposed the change.
- Schlafly argued that ERA would lead to women in combat, greater abortion rates, unisex bathrooms and homosexual marriages.
- The campaign was successful – the ERA failed to become part of the US Constitution because not enough states voted for it.

The 'Roe v Wade' case, 1973

- The campaign to legalise abortion was a key feminist crusade.
- In the famous 'Roe v Wade' court case, lawyers argued successfully that 21-year-old Jane Roe (real name

Norma McCorvey) had the right to an abortion. She had already had two children, both of whom had been put up for adoption.

- In 1973, the Supreme Court ruled that women in all states had the right to safe and legal abortion, overriding the anti-abortion laws of many states.

SUMMARY

- The New Frontier and Great Society were domestic programmes introduced by Presidents Kennedy and Johnson.
- The programmes tried to eliminate poverty and inequality, improve education and fight unemployment.
- Several new organisations worked to improve women's rights, collectively called the 'feminist movement'.
- There were several notable reforms in women's rights, such as the 1972 Educational Amendment Act. However, the Equal Rights Amendment failed to become part of the Constitution.
- After the 'Roe v Wade' case of 1973, women had the right to safe and legal abortion.

 APPLY

DESCRIBE

a Briefly explain how the following made an impact on the women's rights movement:

- NOW
- Equal Rights Amendment (ERA)
- 'Stop ERA'
- 'Roe v Wade' case.

b (EXAM QUESTION) Describe two ways in which people tried to achieve equal rights for women in the early 1960s.

EXAMINER TIP

This question focuses on how people tried to make change happen. You must write about ways in which the action or campaign tried to achieve equal rights.

INTERPRETATION ANALYSIS

a Look at these interpretations about the feminist movement in America.

▼ **INTERPRETATION A** *A female filmmaker speaking in the 2013 film* Feminist: Stories from Women's Liberation; *she was a teenager in the 1970s:*

> Imagine an America where women had the right to vote but could be rejected for a job because of their gender. Imagine an America where women were refused admission to colleges and denied access to credit cards. Imagine being a teacher and being fired for being pregnant. This is what America was like before the Women's Liberation Movement of the 1960s and 1970s. The Women's Liberation Movement changed women's lives socially, economically, and politically. It was described as 'the revolution that will affect everybody'. And it did.

▼ **INTERPRETATION B** *Adapted from a 2001 magazine article by Barbara Epstein, a Social History professor at the University of California who completed her graduate degree during the 1960s:*

> Despite the dramatic accomplishments of the women's movement, gender equality has not yet been achieved. Many more women work outside the home but most continue to be concentrated in low-paying jobs; women earn, on the average, considerably less than men; women are much more likely than men to be poor. Responsibility for childcare remains largely the responsibility of women. In the 1960s and 1970s feminists protested the imbalance in power between men and women in family and personal relations. But these continue to exist.

b (EXAM QUESTION)
1 How does **Interpretation B** differ from **Interpretation A** about the feminist movement? Explain your answer using **Interpretations A** and **B**.

2 Why might the authors of **Interpretations A** and **B** have a different interpretation about the feminist movement?

3 Which interpretation do you find more convincing about the feminist movement? Explain your answer using **Interpretations A** and **B** and your contextual knowledge.

Exam practice

GCSE sample answers

 **REVIEW**

On these exam practice pages you will find a sample student answer for each of the question types you will find in the America section of your Paper 1 exam. What are the strengths and weaknesses of the answers? Read the following pages and think carefully about what the student has written, what the examiner has said about each answer, and how you might improve your own answers to the America exam questions.

Interpretation analysis questions

Paper 1, Section A begins with three questions that ask you to work with two interpretations and their accompanying provenance (caption or label).

The interpretations in Paper 1 are by people who have lived through the events they are referring to. They are speaking at least five years after the events have taken place.

You will be asked three interpretations questions:

- The first question asks *how* the interpretations differ.
- The second question asks you to explain *why* they might differ.
- The third question asks you to *evaluate* what each interpretation has to say about the history involved.

INTERPRETATION ANALYSIS

▼ **INTERPRETATION A** *From* The Roosevelt I Knew *by Frances Perkins (1946); Perkins was a member of the Democratic Party and Secretary of Labour in Roosevelt's New Deal government:*

> The New Deal meant that ordinary people would have a better chance in life. Roosevelt understood that the suffering of the Depression had fallen on those people least able to bear it. He knew that the rich had been hard hit too, but at least they had something left. But the ordinary shopkeeper, the ordinary householder, the farmer who worked the soil himself, the man who worked for wages – these people were desperate. The idea was that all these forces of the community should be directed by making life better for ordinary people.

▼ **INTERPRETATION B** *Adapted from a speech by S.B. Fuller in 1980; he was a self-made, African-American businessman and a Republican:*

> The New Deal of Franklin Roosevelt hurt us. He was a rich man's son. All he received was given to him. So he thinks it's right to give. He didn't understand that when you give to people, you hurt them. We had soup lines and the Depression because men lost confidence in themselves. A dog you feed will not hunt. If you want a dog who hunts, you have to let him get hungry. You're free to eat if you pay for your food, and you're free to starve if you don't.

EXAM QUESTION **1** How does **Interpretation B** differ from **Interpretation A** about President Roosevelt's New Deal? **4 marks**

EXAMINER TIP

While reading the interpretations, try to think about the key point each one makes and how they differ. Making notes around them or underlining the things that are different is excellent preparation for the first of the three questions.

EXAMINER TIP

This question is very straightforward. The examiner will be looking to see if you understand the differences between the two interpretations.

Now look at a student answer. Remember, this question is asking you to write about the ways in which the two interpretations are different.

Sample student answer

Interpretation A focuses on the positive side of Roosevelt and the New Deal. The writer says that Roosevelt realised that ordinary people, such as shopkeepers and farmers, really suffered during the Depression and were desperate. She says that the rich suffered too, but they had some money left while ordinary people didn't.

Interpretation B says bad things about the New Deal.

EXAMINER TIP

The student broadly identifies the differences – that the writer of Interpretation A supported the New Deal, while the author of Interpretation B didn't.

EXAMINER TIP

The student is weaker when analysing Interpretation B and simply writes that they say bad things about the New Deal. The student might have identified that the two people differ in their attitude to Roosevelt's response to the Depression. The author of Interpretation B criticises Roosevelt and feels that he was wrong to simply give people what they needed, rather than make them work for it.

OVERALL COMMENT

This would achieve a Level 1 mark for recognising the contrast with Interpretation B, but it mostly restates the wording of the interpretation.

 2 Why might the authors of **Interpretations A** and **B** have a different interpretation about President Roosevelt's New Deal? Explain your answer using **Interpretations A** and **B** and your contextual knowledge. **4 marks**

EXAMINER TIP

It is really important to think about some possible reasons why the two interpretations might differ. Remember that an interpretation is a person's view about something at least five years after they have lived through it. There will be reasons why they hold that particular view – you need to identify this for the second of the three questions. Read the provenance for each of the interpretations carefully – it will contain clues as to why the person thinks a certain way.

EXAMINER TIP

It is vital that you look at who the author is, the time they were writing or speaking, their intentions and intended audience. You'll never really know why they said what they said, so you must speculate. However, your answer can still be historically informed. Don't repeat *what* is different in the two interpretations (that was question 1) – just focus on *why*!

Look at the student answer. Remember, this question is asking you to write about *why* the interpretations are different. As a result, you will have to read the provenance very carefully.

Sample student answer

The author of Interpretation A focuses on the positive side of the New Deal, probably because she was a member of Roosevelt's own political party, the Democrats. As his Secretary of Labour in his New Deal government, she is far more likely to say positive things about the New Deal.

The author of Interpretation B criticises the way the New Deal worked and feels that it was wrong to simply give money and jobs to people. The author of the Interpretation might feel this way because of their political beliefs as a Republican so he will have different beliefs

EXAMINER TIP

The student uses conditional words such as 'probably', 'more likely' and 'might'. Such a speculative approach is good when not all the facts are known.

EXAMINER TIP

You do not need to restate the difference between the interpretations at the start of your answer. You will have already done this in question 1.

to Roosevelt. He probably believes in laissez-faire – that governments shouldn't interfere too much in people's lives or running businesses. The New Deal did this a lot, so they would not support it. Also, as a self-made businessman, the author achieved success without much help. He objects to the help that the New Deal gives people, arguing that this makes people lose confidence in their own abilities and kills initiative.

EXAMINER TIP

The student uses their contextual knowledge of the period here by outlining the Republican belief in laissez-faire.

OVERALL COMMENT

This is a low Level 2 answer. It is weaker on Interpretation A – the answer needs to explore the views of Frances Perkins in more detail. For example, the student should explore why, as Secretary of State for Labour, she would want the New Deal to be seen positively.

 EXAM QUESTION **3** Which interpretation do you find more convincing about President Roosevelt's New Deal? Explain your answer using **Interpretations A** and **B** and your contextual knowledge.

8 marks

EXAMINER TIP

Of the three interpretation questions, the final one is worth most marks. Make sure you leave enough time to answer this one carefully, ensuring that you evaluate both interpretations in detail before arriving at your judgement.

This question uses the key word 'convincing'. So, your answer should focus not on the differences or the provenance of the two interpretations, but on the history surrounding the issue in the question – here, 'President Roosevelt's New Deal'.

In simple terms, you are being asked which interpretation is better – which one 'fits in' with what you have learned. One way to look at it is to think of the two interpretations as witnesses in a trial – which version, based on all you have learned about the topic, is most believable (or 'convincing')? Now look at the student answer.

Sample student answer

Firstly, Interpretation A is quite convincing because I know that the New Deal helped many ordinary people such as shopkeepers, homeowners and farmers who were hit hard by the Depression. For example, the FCA (Farm Credit Administration) lent money to farmers who couldn't keep up with loan payments. $100 million was loaned out in 18 months. Also, the CWA (Civil Works Administration) provided temporary work for 4 million men, building schools, airports and roads. The theory behind the New Deal was to 'prime the pump' of the economy. The government created jobs by spending money and once the workers earned wages, they would start buying goods. Firms and businesses would then start hiring new workers and these new workers would spend money and so on. I also know that people were desperate during the Depression because around 13 million people had lost their jobs by 1932 and 20,000 companies went out of business. Around 250,000 Americans stopped paying their mortgages in 1932 alone and most were evicted from their homes. Also, by 1932, one in 20 farmers had been evicted.

EXAMINER TIP

The student backs up their answers with fact-based examples. However, while the information supplied at the end of this paragraph is good knowledge about the Depression and its impact, it is not about the New Deal. The student would need to explain how the New Deal helped these people.

OVERALL COMMENT

This answer would reach Level 3 if it provided good historical knowledge in support of both interpretations.

OVER TO YOU

Read the sample answers again, but this time:

a In Answer 1, highlight where it specifically mentions the *differences* between the two interpretations.

b In Answer 2, highlight where it gives reasons *why* the two interpretations are different.

c For Answer 3, write a paragraph about Interpretation B, and a conclusion that gives evidence to support your choice.

d Finally, have a go at writing a series of answers yourself, making sure you closely follow the advice given here. You should spend about 5 minutes on question 1, 5 minutes on question 2 and 10 minutes on question 3.

The 'describe' question

 EXAM QUESTION

4 Describe two ways in which Prohibition had an impact on society.

4 marks

Sample student answer

There are many ways that Prohibition had an impact on society. One impact was that Prohibition led to a rise in organised crime. Criminal gangs ran illegal bars called speakeasies, which sold bootleg alcohol smuggled in from abroad by bootleggers. The gangs did not just get involved in the illegal alcohol trade. They also made money through fixing horse and dog racing, running brothels and racketeering.

Another impact on society was the corruption of law enforcement and a decline in respect for the law.

OVERALL COMMENT

This answer would achieve a low Level 2 for identifying and explaining the first impact. The key to reaching the higher marks is ensuring that you explain two ways.

OVER TO YOU

1 Now it's time for you to have a go at planning and writing an answer to this question. Spend no more than 5 minutes on your answer.

2 Now check your answer.

☐ Did you name two ways in which Prohibition had an impact?

☐ For each one, did you *expand* on it and *say why* it had an impact on society?

The 'in what ways' question

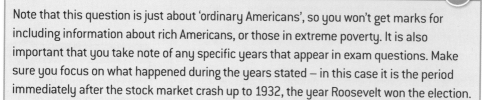

5 In what ways did the lives of ordinary Americans change because of the Depression, 1929–1932?

8 marks

EXAMINER TIP

The 'in what ways' question is not an essay question – the aim is that you quickly write down the ways in which the lives of the vast majority of ordinary Americans *changed* during the early years of the Depression.

EXAMINER TIP

Note that this question is just about 'ordinary Americans', so you won't get marks for including information about rich Americans, or those in extreme poverty. It is also important that you take note of any specific years that appear in exam questions. Make sure you focus on what happened during the years stated – in this case it is the period immediately after the stock market crash up to 1932, the year Roosevelt won the election.

Sample student answer

The lives of ordinary Americans changed a lot because of the Depression between 1929 and 1932. Before the Depression hit America, the 1920s was a time of economic boom in the US. The vast majority of businesses were doing well, sales were high, wages were on the increase and unemployment was low. In the early 1930s, the Depression caused a number of economic and social changes.

For example, in the early 1930s, unemployment rose rapidly. Around 13 million people had lost their jobs by 1932, nearly 25 per cent of the labour force. Between 1929 and 1932, factory production dropped by 45 per cent and house-building fell by 80 per cent. By 1932, 20,000 companies had gone out of business.

In 1932, around 250,000 Americans stopped paying their mortgages and many were evicted from their homes. Some took to living on the streets or moved to urban waste ground where communities built shacks with boxes, scrap metal, old cloth and pallets, called Hoovervilles. Charities set up soup kitchens where the homeless could get soup and bread and the huge queues that formed were known as breadlines.

A further change that took place was an increase in social unrest, violence and protest. For example, poor farmers in Iowa used guns and pitchforks to chase away government officials who tried to evict farm owners who couldn't pay their mortgages. And in summer 1932, 25,000 unemployed ex-soldiers marched to Washington DC and asked for their war pension (or 'bonus') to be paid early. In response, President Hoover set the army on them, who drove the 'Bonus Army' away with guns, tanks and tear-gas.

EXAMINER TIP

The student briefly mentions what the US was like before the onset of the Depression, in the 1920s. This allows the student to really focus on the changes that took place as a result of the onset of the Depression.

EXAMINER TIP

The student uses examples to illustrate the points they are making. They also use the correct terms, such as Hooverville and breadlines, for example.

EXAMINER TIP

The student has written about a number of ways in which the Depression of the early 1930s changed the lives of ordinary Americans.

OVERALL COMMENT

This answer would achieve Level 3 for its detailed knowledge of the way the lives of ordinary Americans changed because of the Depression. It could achieve Level 4 if it recognised not just the different effects on different groups of people, but the fact that some people were not affected at all by the onset of the Depression.

OVER TO YOU

1 How would you improve the sample answer?

2 Now it's time for you to have a go at planning and writing an answer to this question. Spend about 10 minutes on your answer.

3 Now check your answer.

☐ Did you name at least two ways in which the lives of ordinary Americans changed because of the Depression?

☐ For each change, did you add a few details based on your own knowledge (facts) and understanding to explain why it had an impact?

The 'bullet points' question

> 6 Which of the following made America a better, fairer society:
> - Kennedy's New Frontier
> - Johnson's Great Society?
>
> Explain your answer with reference to both events. **12 marks**

Sample student answer

Kennedy's New Frontier tried to make America a better, fairer society, but it had limited success. For example, JFK supported the Civil Rights Movement and gave important government jobs to African-Americans. The CEEO (Commission on Equal Employment Opportunity) was created during Kennedy's presidency to ensure that all people employed with the federal government had equal employment opportunities. However, the CEEO only helped those who already had a government job and did nothing to actively find jobs for millions of unemployed African-Americans. Kennedy was also accused of being too concerned with what Southern politicians and voters thought of him – and actually tried to get Martin Luther King to call off his great march to Washington DC. With the economy, JFK had a number of successes, such as making $900 million available to businesses to create new jobs, increasing spending on the armed forces to create jobs and giving grants to companies to buy high-tech equipment and train their workers to use it. However, the new equipment sometimes meant that fewer workers were needed, so some people lost their jobs. Also, many new jobs were dependent on government spending, which made them vulnerable to spending cuts.

Johnson's Great Society also tried to make America a fairer, better society – and in some cases it had more success than the New Frontier. For example, the Civil Rights Act of 1964 and the Voting Rights Act of 1965 were introduced during LBJ's presidency, and the Immigration Act ended racial quotas for people entering the USA. In education, 'Operation Headstart' gave money to schools in cities to provide a better education for the poor and the Elementary and Secondary Education Act provided major funding for schools. The Job Corps was introduced to help high school leavers get jobs and the Volunteers In Service To

EXAMINER TIP

The aim of the bullet points question is to get you to show that you know about the reasons, events and consequences of the period in American history that you have studied. You might be asked to focus on results, impacts or causes. This particular question focuses on two major domestic programmes introduced by Presidents Kennedy and Johnson in the 1960s. You will also have to reach a judgement (conclusion) that relates to the question.

EXAMINER TIP

This answer goes into detail about JFK's New Frontier. It highlights the successes and failures of JFK's work on civil rights, the economy and education.

EXAMINER TIP

The student shows detailed knowledge and good understanding of LBJ's Great Society and its impact on US society. The student has not wasted time by writing about things that are not related to the bullet points. They simply deal with the New Frontier and the Great Society.

America (VISTA) programme was set up as a domestic version of the Peace Corps. In response to problems in healthcare and poverty, the era of the Great Society saw the minimum wage increase, a Housing Act fund low-income housing and a Model Cities Act clear up inner-city slums. 'Medicare', which was actually a JFK idea, was eventually created to fund healthcare for the elderly and low-income families.

In conclusion, I think Johnson's Great Society had the greatest impact.

EXAMINER TIP

This conclusion is weak. The student needs to give reasons *why* they thought Johnson's Great Society had greater impact than Kennedy's New Frontier.

OVERALL COMMENT

This answer would achieve Level 3. A conclusion similar to the following would have helped the answer achieve a Level 4:

I think that Johnson's Great Society had the greater impact in making America a better, fairer society because it actually put into practice many of the ideas that JFK was unable to do. While JFK's New Frontier contained many great ideas, he was often unable to make them happen because politicians from the South refused to support his plans. Kennedy was a well-polished politician, whereas LBJ was an intimidating, tough-talking veteran. As a Southerner he could relate to the concerns of the Southern politicians and managed to push through far-reaching reforms such as the Civil Rights Act of 1964, the Voting Rights Act of 1965 and 'Medicare'.

EXAMINER TIP

Note how this conclusion makes links between the New Frontier and the Great Society.

OVER TO YOU

1 Reread the sample answer. Highlight in different colours where it mentions:
   - the way in which JFK's New Frontier made America a better, fairer society
   - the way in which LBJ's Great Society made America a better, fairer society.

   Underline the sentences where the student gives reasons why they think one of the bullet points made America a better, fairer society than the other.

2 Have a go at writing your own rough essay plan to the question – you could use bullet points. You only have 15 minutes on this question, so don't spend more than 4 minutes creating the rough plan. Check your plan.

   ☐ Did you plan what you will say for each of the two bullet points?

   ☐ Did you come to a quick decision (judgement) about whether the New Frontier or the Great society made America a better, fairer society?

   ☐ Did you note down one or two reasons *why* one of those bullet points had a greater impact on US society? (Remember, explaining why you came to your conclusion would help you get higher marks.)

   ☐ Did you manage to complete your plan within a few minutes?

3 Use your essay plan to answer this question.

The answers provided here are examples, based on the information in the Recap sections of this Revision Guide. There may be other factors which are relevant to each question, and you should draw on as much of your own knowledge as possible to give detailed and precise answers. There are also many ways of answering exam questions (for example, of structuring an essay). However, these exemplar answers offer a good starting point.

Chapter 1 Page 13
DESCRIBE

a
- American constitution: the system of laws and basic principles that governs America.
- Bill of Rights: part of the constitution, outlining the rights and freedoms of US citizens.
- Republican Party: more likely to preserve traditions. Followed a policy of 'laissez-faire'. Against high taxes. Strong support in North.
- Democratic Party: more likely to intervene in everyday life, helping the most vulnerable. Strong support in South.

b
- Similarities: Both are types of government in the US. Both have elected officials that govern on behalf of the people.
- Differences: Central government oversees matters that affect the whole country; state government creates state laws and has its own police and court system, and its own governor.

Page 15
IN WHAT WAYS

a
- Economic boom: a period when the vast majority of businesses are doing well, sales are high, wages increase and unemployment is low.
- Consumer society: when increased wages mean people can buy goods that they did not have before or have been recently invented.

b Answer might include:
- First World War: *Two facts:* America sold goods to the fighting countries; war disrupted the economic growth of those countries, and America began to fill the gap in the market. *How did it contribute?:* Demand for US goods created jobs. The fact that the USA was not as affected by war meant that it could take over markets that were once occupied by countries such as Germany and Britain.

- New consumer goods: *Two facts:* More homes with electricity; more demand for electric powered goods. *How did it contribute?:* Demand for these goods created jobs in factories.
- Mass production: *Two facts:* Developed in the car industry; goods got cheaper as companies got better and quicker at making them. *How did it contribute?:* Jobs were created in steel, glass, leather and rubber industries as a result of growth in car manufacturing.
- Advertising: *Two facts:* Billboards, newspapers and magazines urged people to buy the latest gadgets; catalogues were produced, and goods delivered to your door. *How did it contribute?:* People tried to keep up with their neighbours so it led to a boost in sales.
- 'Buy now, pay later': *Two facts:* Sometimes called a 'hire purchase plan'; consumers could pay for goods in small instalments over a fixed period. *How did it contribute?:* Easier to buy expensive goods, leading to boost in sales.
- Import duties: *Two facts:* Tax on goods coming into USA; made foreign goods more expensive. *How did it contribute?:* Encouraged people to buy US-made goods.
- Low taxes: *Two facts:* Republican policy; people had more to spend. *How did it contribute?:* People bought more goods.
- 'Laissez-faire': *Two facts:* Means 'leave alone'; Republican policy. *How did it contribute?:* Businesses could concentrate on creating wealth.

c You may write about the improved prospects of finding employment as a result of the boom and the increase in consumer goods available to buy. Goods began to get cheaper as a result of mass production methods, and the success of the motor industry affected related industries such as steel and leather – more jobs were created in these industries as more cars were made. You might also mention the impact of the new electric-powered 'gadgets' (e.g. vacuum cleaners, radios), several of which were labour-saving devices, which created more time for leisure, e.g. going to the cinema.

Page 17
DESCRIBE

a
- Stock market: a place where shares could be bought and sold.

- Investor: a person who puts money into something to make a profit.
- Shareholder: a person who owns part (or a share) of a company.
- Dividend: a share of the company profits.
- 'buying on margin': shares bought with 10% deposit; the rest is paid with profits when shares are sold.

b A shareholder buys shares (sometimes by borrowing from a bank). They make money by either receiving a share of the company profits (a dividend) each year or selling their share for more than they paid for it.

INTERPRETATION ANALYSIS

a Ford introduced the assembly line – an electric conveyor belt that carried the partly assembled car past workers who did one or two small jobs repeatedly, such as fitting wheels or doors. It meant the cars could be made quicker and cheaper.

c 1 A: very positive about Ford; sees him as a 'God' because of his control.
B: negative view of Ford; viewed Ford as someone who was so obsessed with control that he hired people to hurt workers who were not happy at Ford Motor Company, and had thought about forming a union to complain; suggests workers were not highly regarded, were intimidated, and were considered expendable.

2 A: Red Cole was a loyal employee; as an 18-year-old he liked the money, work, and pride in the association with Ford and his modern mass production methods; work was regular, ordered, well paid and he had a positive view as a result.
B: Herndon was a journalist, and would make money from selling a book which people would buy if it said new and controversial things, he is making comments about Ford who was a legendary figure in American business, as a journalist he may be a supporter of unions, Ford was by now dead.

Page 19
DESCRIBE

a This is when the wealth of the population is not evenly spread, so some have great wealth while others live in poverty. For example, there were an estimated 15,000 millionaires in the US in 1927, yet 6 million families (42% of the total) had an income of less than $1000 a year.

b Write your own revision cards.

c You might write about farmers – incomes dropped because they produced more than they could sell and there was a drop in demand in Europe. By the early 1930s, farmers were only earning a third of their income in 1920. They could not repay loans so many had to sell their farms to raise money or were evicted from their land. In 1924 alone, 600,000 farmers lost their farms. You might also write about African-American workers. Many worked on Southern farms as labourers or sharecroppers. As farming suffered in general, African-American farmworkers and sharecroppers were hit particularly hard as they were already very poor. Many moved to cities to find work but could often only find low-paid jobs.

Chapter 2 Page 21
INTERPRETATION ANALYSIS

a Morton's grandmother said Jelly Roll had brought shame on the family by playing jazz. She said jazz was 'devil music' and would be his downfall.

b She was part of an older generation that disapproved of this new form of entertainment because it was seen to encourage drunkenness and immorality. She feared that Jelly Roll Morton would ruin his life ('bring about my downfall') through playing jazz. As his grandmother she cared about him and his future.

DESCRIBE

a Answer might include:
- Jazz music: Fact 1: Originated in the Southern states among African-Americans. Fact 2: Louis Armstrong, Duke Ellington and Bessie Smith were popular jazz musicians.
- Cinema: Fact 1: Weekly audiences grew from 35 million in 1919 to 100 million in 1930. Fact 2: *The Jazz Singer* (1927) was the first 'talkie'.
- Sport: Fact 1: Babe Ruth (baseball) and Bobby Jones (golf) became celebrities. Fact 2: Radio broadcasts and newspapers brought sporting events to a mass audience.
- Crazes: Fact 1: Marathon dancing was popular – people would see how long they could dance without stopping. Fact 2: Mahjong and crosswords were popular pastimes.

b 'Roaring' implies that things were going well, and people were having a great time. It was a time of having fun and loud music, wild parties and new forms of entertainment.

c You should use your answer to **a** as the basis of your answer.

Page 23
IN WHAT WAYS

a Flappers were the independent and fashionable young women of the 1920s. They had short, bobbed hairstyles and wore lots of make-up. They dressed in short skirts, revealing tops and wore silk stockings rolled to just above the knee. They smoked cigarettes and drank alcohol in public. They held their dance partners close without wearing gloves and some of them had sex before marriage.

b
- Women before the First World War: Fact 1: Led restricted lives. Fact 2: Could not vote. Fact 3: Middle- and upper-class women were expected to behave politely at all times and wear sensible clothing.
- Women during the war: Fact 1: Took over the jobs of the men who went away to fight. Fact 2: The money they earned gave them a sense of independence. Fact 3: They worked just as hard and as well as men.
- Women after the war: Fact 1: American women were given the right to vote in 1920. Fact 2: Less likely to stay in an unhappy marriage – the divorce rate doubled during the 1920s. Fact 3: Flappers became a common sight.

c For the vast majority of US women, life went on as usual. They were too busy working or raising families to go to wild parties, and could not afford luxuries. Despite gaining the vote, during the 1920s women were still not equal to men. They tended to work in the least skilled jobs and earned less than men in the same job.

d Before the First World War women led restricted lives. They couldn't vote, and were expected to behave politely at all times and wear sensible clothing. Poorer women had to settle for poorly paid jobs such as cleaning, low-skilled factory work and secretarial work. In the war, women took over the jobs of fighting men. Money they earned gave them a sense of independence. US women were given the vote in 1920, partly because of war work. By 1929, there were around 10.5 million women with jobs, around 25% more than in 1920. With money of their own, women could choose to live alone, and were less likely to stay in a bad marriage – the divorce rate doubled during the 1920s. With fewer restrictions, some women began

to behave and dress differently. Flappers wore more revealing clothes, went on dates unchaperoned and smoked and drank in public.

BULLET POINTS

You will need to demonstrate a range of accurate knowledge and understanding of both bullets. You should write that the cultural changes – jazz music, cinema, sport – had a major impact on America, and so too did social changes – the role and position of women, immigration, increased wealth as a result of the Boom. Higher level answers should link the two bullets – for example, the rise in popularity of jazz (cultural) provided great opportunities for black musicians (social).

Chapter 3 Page 25
IN WHAT WAYS

a
- Prohibition: ban on alcohol in the USA from 1920 to 1933.
- Bootlegging: smuggling alcohol across the border.
- Speakeasy: illegal bars selling bootleg alcohol.
- Moonshine: strong, home-made alcohol.
- Organised crime: gangs involved in the illegal alcohol trade and other crimes.
- Gangster: a member of an organised crime gang.

b *Why Prohibition was introduced*: Moral reasons – it was argued that alcohol contributed to a decline in moral values, America would be a better, healthier place if alcohol was banned. Religious reasons – religious organisations and churches claimed alcohol caused a variety of social problems such as violence, poverty, addiction and debt. Patriotic reasons – Americans who drank imported German beer could be seen as traitors. Rural America – people in rural areas saw the growing towns and cities as places where alcohol-fuelled violence and crime were commonplace. Pressure groups like the Anti-Saloon League led strong campaigns.

Why prohibition failed: Prohibition agents could not prevent alcohol being smuggled in by sea or over the borders with Canada and Mexico. It was difficult to enforce prohibition on a public that wanted to drink. It was very easy to get alcohol because criminal gangs got involved in its manufacture and supply. The gangs made so much money they could avoid arrest and prosecution by bribing police officers, Prohibition agents, border guards and judges.

c Before Prohibition, alcohol was widely available in many states. However, there was an influential campaign to introduce national Prohibition based on moral, political and religious reasons. When Prohibition was introduced there was:

- a rise in organised crime: Gangs satisfied demand for alcohol through bootlegging, moonshine and speakeasies. There were approximately 200,000 speakeasies in the US by 1933.
- loss of respect for lawmakers: Organised crime made so much money that gangsters could avoid arrest and prosecution by bribing some police officers, Prohibition agents, border guards and judges.

Page 27
INTERPRETATION ANALYSIS

b • **A** = feels hated in his new home. Sarcastically references things that Americans refer to as a benefit of living there: liberty, democracy, rights. Words: do you want to know the truth?, hatred, contemptuous.

- **B** = in awe of America, feels it is a land of opportunity for everyone. Words: grand, amazing, fantastic, exciting, pots of money.

c **1** **A** is negative about his experience in the USA. He says that the US is known for 'democracy', 'rights' and 'liberty' but that is not the whole story and many Americans feel hatred towards immigrants. **B** is very positive about the US, saying that it is a land of opportunity, even for ordinary people. **A** has lived in America, whereas **B** is talking about what he has heard about the immigrant experience.

2 The two differ because **A** has lived there and had a negative experience, while **B** had not yet been there and based his idea of America on what others told him.

DESCRIBE

a • The 'new' immigrants were usually poor, couldn't speak English well and had unfamiliar traditions and religious practices. Many 'new' immigrants were Jewish or Catholic, whereas most of the established immigrants were Protestants.

- The First World War had added to the suspicions many Americans had of 'foreigners', especially Russian immigrants.

- There was a feeling that the immigrants were out to 'steal' jobs because they were willing to work for very low wages in any kind of job.
- The immigrants tended to live in ethnic communities, which could have given the impression that they were not mixing.

b A series of laws – in 1917, 1920 and 1924 (the Literacy Act, Immigration Quota Law and National Origins Act).

c Answer might include:

- Working and living conditions were generally very poor and immigrants suffered considerable hardship.
- Accusations of being out to steal jobs created tension.
- Difficulties in getting extended family members from abroad to join them as a result of immigration laws.
- Continued persecution as a result of unfamiliar traditions and religious practices.
- Homesickness for their home country and relatives left behind.

Page 29
IN WHAT WAYS

a • Segregation: when African-Americans were kept separate from white Americans

- Jim Crow Laws: a series of racist laws that tried to uphold segregation
- Black 'Renaissance': a time of creativity, black culture and pride among African-Americans, especially in Harlem, New York.

b Most members were poor white people in rural parts of Southern and Western states. They had not seen the same prosperity as the wealthier, Northern states. They looked for someone to blame for this and felt that African-Americans and immigrant workers left many white people out of work. They saw themselves as 'defenders' of their Protestant religion and moral standards. The Klan's secrecy, with its coded language, menacing hooded costume and strange rituals, was part of the appeal for many who joined.

c You should write that while black Americans continued to face widespread discrimination, particularly in the southern states as a result of the Jim Crow laws and a corrupt legal system, many headed north and enjoyed better pay and increased opportunities in industry and entertainment. However, they still received

wages considerably lower than white workers, and worsening racial tensions led to some race riots.

Yet some African-American communities flourished in the northern cities. Harlem, New York, became a centre for creativity, black culture and black pride because of the work of talented black poets, writers, artists and musicians. Some called this the black 'Renaissance'. There were political changes too: in 1910, WEB Du Bois – the great-grandson of an African slave – set up the NAACP, the National Association for the Advancement of Colored People, which worked hard to improve the rights of African-Americans, such as campaigning for the right to vote.

Page 31
BULLET POINTS

a You should create your own revision cards for this activity.

b You should explain both the impact of the KKK and the impact of the Red Scare. You might write about each of these factors in isolation and then try to link the two, including the fact that they are both examples of intolerance in the USA at this time. Both bullet points highlight the limitations to the 'land of opportunity'; it was not a land of opportunity for all African-Americans or immigrants.

The best answers will also discuss the different, and greater, impact on different groups within US society in different places, for example in the Southern states (KKK) or in the Northern urban centres (the Red Scare).

Chapter 4 Page 33
DESCRIBE

a • overproduction: producing goods faster than they can be sold
- foreign tariffs: a tax placed on a good coming into the country to make it more expensive
- profit: a financial gain – the difference between the amount earned and the amount spent on buying something

b Possible content for a flow diagram:
- There were huge **inequalities of wealth** in the US and some couldn't afford the goods that were produced.
- US industry was **overproducing**, so many goods remained unsold.
- Not as many goods were sold abroad because foreign governments put **taxes (or tariffs) on US-made goods**, making them more expensive.

- Some **began to doubt whether the companies in which they had invested would keep making large profits** and began to sell their shares.
- This concern spread as people **began to 'panic sell' their shares**.
- On 24 October 1929 (**Black Thursday**), 13 million shares were sold on the New York Stock Exchange and share prices in nearly all companies began to drop.
- On **Tuesday 29 October**, there was another mad panic to sell shares and shareholders lost a total of $8 billion.
- Many Americans had borrowed money from banks to buy shares, but now they couldn't pay back the loans and the **banks went bankrupt**.

c There were inequalities of wealth – not all Americans could afford the goods that the factories produced and there was a limit to the number of goods people could buy – so American factories were overproducing, and profits were beginning to fall. Also, companies were struggling to sell their goods abroad because foreign governments had put taxes (or tariffs) on US-made goods. These countries wanted to encourage their citizens to buy goods made in their own country. As a result, America sold fewer goods abroad and this began to hit US companies hard.

Page 35
INTERPRETATION ANALYSIS

a
- Hooverville: waste land where people built homes from scrap
- Breadline: line of people queuing up to get donations of soup and bread
- Hobo: jobless person who moved around the country looking for work.

c 1 **Interpretation A** shows negative effects: the author has lost his job and savings. It also mentions the great impact on others, especially widows. **Interpretation B** suggests that the impact wasn't great: people still drove expensive cars, no breadlines, 1930s was 'glittering' – no visible signs of poverty.

2 Authors are from different ends of the social spectrum – working class versus rich family background.

3 Focus on which one fits best with what you have learned. You will probably go with **A**, backing up your opinion with factual knowledge. The author of **A** is a worker (and most Americans were workers) and his job meant he saw the broad impact. **B** is more closed in his world of privilege.

IN WHAT WAYS

a Effects could include: Farmers were evicted from their farms (social and economic); people lost their savings when the banks closed (social and economic); banks went bankrupt (economic); people were forced to live in Hoovervilles (social).

b Answers might include:
- Millions of investors lost a fortune; they tried to pay back bank loans by selling valuables, but some struggled to pay rent and faced homelessness. Some lived in Hoovervilles and relied on handouts on breadlines.
- Factory owners were forced to cut production, then wages, and eventually to sack workers. Local businesses were affected by a drop in trade. Around 13 million people had lost their jobs by 1932, nearly 25% of the labour force. By 1932, 20,000 companies closed.
- Banks closed when borrowers couldn't repay loans. Staff lost their jobs and savers lost their savings.
- Farmers with equipment loans now had to pay back the money – some couldn't afford to pay their debts and faced losing their farms.

Page 37
BULLET POINTS

a
- Background: *Hoover:* Self-made man – orphaned aged eight; made his fortune in the mining industry; multi-millionaire by the age of 40. *FDR:* From a wealthy, well-connected family; privately educated.
- Political party: *Hoover:* Republican, believed in idea of laissez-faire. *FDR:* Democrat, despite tradition of Republicans in his family. His wife cared deeply about the poor and the Democrats were traditionally favoured by poorer voters.
- Political career: *Hoover:* Excellent early career in politics, especially during the First World War. Elected president in 1928. *FDR:* Helped organise the navy during the First World War; contracted polio in 1921 which confined him to wheelchair. Re-entered politics in 1928, becoming Governor of New York.
- Ideas for dealing with the Depression: *Hoover:* Thought of Americans as 'rugged individuals', able to overcome any problem without help and through hard work. Did little to begin with. Eventually he lent money to troubled businesses

---

and farms, made cash available to states to help unemployed and began large-scale construction projects. *FDR:* Spent $20 million of tax money helping the unemployed as Governor of NY. Promised America the '3 Rs' – Relief, Recovery and Reform as part of a 'New Deal'.

b
- Laissez-faire: The idea that the state should not interfere with people's lives. *Impact in election* Hoover's response to the Depression was seen as too little, too late.
- 'New Deal': FDR's phrase relating to what he promised the American people. *Impact in election* Seen as something new and different from what Hoover was doing, so it attracted voters.
- Rugged individualism: The idea that Americans can get over problems by working hard and without government intervention. *Impact in election* Made Hoover look uncaring and unwilling to help, so attracted fewer votes.
- '3 Rs': FDR's promises – relief, recovery, reform. *Impact in election* He looked like he was actively trying to improve the situation – very different from Hoover.

c You should both define and explain how the policies of both laissez-faire and rugged individualism had a negative effect on Hoover's campaign and how FDR's campaign benefited from the idea of a New Deal, the concept of the '3 Rs' and the fact that FDR took his message around the country. You might find differences in the campaigns that had an impact on the result – for example, Hoover's poor record of public speaking compared to FDR's warmth as a speaker, or the policies of the two parties.

Chapter 5 Page 39
DESCRIBE

a Two further examples might include:
- Action by FDR: The Economy Act. *Brief explanation:* All government employees had 15% pay cut. *How it helped the country:* Saved $1 billion, which could then be spent on the New Deal. *Criticisms or issues?* Some government employees may not have been happy with a wage cut. Republicans may not have been happy that the government was interfering.
- Action by FDR: AAA (Agricultural Adjustment Agency). *Brief explanation:* Paid farmers to produce less. *How it helped the country:* Food prices rose because supply fell. Farmers' incomes

increased, and fewer lost their farms. *Criticisms or issues?* Food was being destroyed when millions in the cities were going hungry.

b • The rich: did not like higher taxes.
  • Business people: the government interference of the New Deal.
  • The Supreme Court: felt that federal government should not be interfering in state matters. It declared many NRA codes illegal.
  • Republicans: believed in laissez-faire and rugged individualism, so did not like interference. Some worried that the government had too much power.

c You should use your answers from **a** and **b** to help you plan and write your response.

Page 41

IN WHAT WAYS

a • Farmer's wife in Tennessee Valley: happy with the TVA and AAA but not particularly benefiting from New Deal policies on women
  • Henry Ford: happy that GNP was rising as more people could afford his cars, and fewer strike days; not so happy with higher taxes, or the meddling of the NRA and trade unions
  • Ford car worker: more cars sold meant more job security; family helped by Alphabet Agencies; happy with right to join union
  • African-American restaurant worker: might have more money to spend they got a job with an Alphabet Agency, but no great change in terms of segregation or discrimination
  • Small-scale farmer in Dust Bowl: no real change; unhappy, might have benefited from agency job, but no real impact from AAA

b Focus your answer on how the New Deal satisfied these objectives – relief (help for the old, sick, unemployed and homeless, e.g. FERA); recovery (government schemes to provide jobs, e.g. CCC); reform (make America a better place for ordinary people and future generations, e.g. TVA). FERA provided soup kitchens, blankets, clothes and nursery school places to those in need; CCC created jobs for 2.5 million 18-25-year-olds; TVA provided work building dams and electric power stations along the Tennessee River, one of America's poorest areas.

c Answer might include: The New Deal created jobs – 2.5 million 18-to 25-year-olds got work in the CCC, and the CWA provided temporary work for 4 million men, building

schools, airports and roads. FDR was 'priming the pump' – once the workers earn wages, they start buying goods, firms and businesses then start hiring new workers who spend money, and so on. Also, the number of bank failures dropped dramatically during the New Deal. The number of days workers went on strike increased in 1934, but by 1938 it had dropped to 1932 levels. Also, Gross National Product (GNP) rose steadily from 1933 to 1941. A rising GNP is seen as a sign that a country is gradually getting wealthier.

INTERPRETATION ANALYSIS

b **1** **Interpretation A** is very positive. The author felt FDR was trying to get the USA back on its feet and thinks things were better due to FDR. **Interpretation B** is negative about FDR and the New Deal, stating that the New Deal meant only higher taxes, and that FDR didn't solve the poverty issue. He implies FDR made things worse, whereas the author of **A** implies things were better.

2 **A** benefited from FDR's New Deal – he lost his job at the start of the Great Depression but got work with the WPA. **B** is a rich American, who was not impacted by the Depression, so only sees FDR as someone who raises taxes and little else.

3 You may judge that **A** is more convincing as it takes a slightly more balanced view – not saying that FDR solved all problems, but tried hard to pull America out of a 'rut', evidenced by laws, schemes, programmes etc. It says things are better than they were, which is evidenced by improving GNP, fewer strikes etc. **B** is quite a narrow view, based on taxation being higher and the fact he didn't help the poverty situation, even though specific Alphabet Agencies were directed at it (FERA).

Page 43

DESCRIBE

a The common ideas, customs and behaviour of a society, including ideas, music, books and the mass media.

b Write your own revision cards.

c Answer might include: new artists such as Glenn Miller, Judy Garland and Bing Crosby, and that music was listened to through the increasingly popular gramophones; new cinema stars and genres – musicals (e.g. *42nd Street*), Walt Disney cartoons, historical dramas (e.g. *Gone with the Wind*) and horror films (e.g. *Frankenstein*

and *Dracula*); comic books, which first appeared in the early 1930s; developments in literature as authors such as Erskine Caldwell, John Steinbeck and James T Farrell wrote about the Depression, poverty, racism and social problems.

INTERPRETATION ANALYSIS

b Alice wouldn't want her children to go to the movies even though she can't afford it because she thinks they are a bad influence. Her preacher disapproves too.

c She lives a traditional, rural life in the South, under the religious influence of a preacher. She wants to retain traditions. She thinks new ideas/influences (like modern dancing and cinema) are wrong and has not embraced the changes of the last few decades.

IN WHAT WAYS

a Answers could include: comic books introduced, gramophone sales rose as vinyl records became more widely available, authors wrote about the Great Depression, WPA existed.

b Answers could include: jazz still popular, and so were some of the same artists, going to the movies remained very popular.

Chapter 6 Page 45

BULLET POINTS

a • Isolationism: US policy to keep out of the affairs of other countries
  • Cash and Carry Plan: November 1939 plan for the US to sell weapons to Britain and France
  • Lend Lease: March 1941 plan for the US to 'lend' weapons to Britain.

b The War Production Board (WPB) was created to convert industries to war work. Factories received all the materials they needed to produce the most war goods in the fastest time.

c The chart might include:
  • Unemployed: *Before the war* Around 9.5 million unemployed Americans. *Impact of the war* Unemployment fell as USA began to rearm. By 1941, around 4 million had jobs in the armed forces or building fighter planes, battleships and tanks. By 1944, unemployment had dropped to 670,000. Employment on farms and in the traditional industries of coal, iron, steel and oil were all boosted by the demands of war.
  • Women: *Before the war* Tended to work in traditional 'female' jobs such as nursing or teaching. *Impact of the war* As millions

of men joined up, women began to fill their places in factories, railways and shipyards. Between 1940 and 1945, the number of women in work rose from 12 million to nearly 19 million. Women now occupied a third of all US jobs.

- African-Americans: *Before the war* Faced severe discrimination, but the government set up the Fair Employment Practice Committee (FEPC) in 1941 to help prevent discrimination against them in defence and government jobs. *Impact of the war* Some companies improved their policies but there was still much discrimination in the armed services (e.g. black sailors could only work in ships' kitchens). As the war went on, racial barriers began to fall, e.g. the air force let African-Americans train as pilots.

c You should use your answer to **c** to help you plan and write your response. You should conclude with which group you think experienced most change.

Chapter 7 Page 47
IN WHAT WAYS

a • Consumerism: the concept that the ever-expanding consumption of goods is beneficial for the economy
- Fair Deal: Truman's attempt to help Americans most in need and bring about a fairer society
- Rock and Roll generation: 1950s teenagers who listened to Rock and Roll and had more leisure time and spending power than previous generations

b Answers might include:
- Once-thriving town and city centres declined as people went 'out-of-town' to shop in new malls.
- Before the war, women worked in traditional 'female' jobs, e.g. nursing. During the war, women took men's places in factories. After the war, most women went back to being housewives.
- You could refer to changes in youth culture, the economy or social conditions.

c You could write about the new era of consumerism, reflected in the availability of luxury goods, such as fridges and vacuum cleaners at affordable prices. Huge malls were built outside large towns and cities to sell the goods. By the end of the 1950s, 9 out of 10 US households had a TV, 8 had a car and a phone and 7 had a washing machine. Confidence in the economy made

people willing to have large families – so the population grew (baby boom). As America grew wealthier, the 'Rock and Roll generation' emerged with more leisure time and spending power than previous generations.

Page 49
BULLET POINTS

a Create your own quiz.

b Answer might include that the impacts are different – one positive and one negative. **McCarthyism:** negative social impact – suspicion, fear, people betraying others, challenges to US constitution. **Changes in US economy:** positive economic impact led to some positive social impacts – improvement in living standards and rising wages, ever-expanding consumption of goods was good for the economy.

You could also compare the impacts: improvements in the economy boosted the desire of some to defend the capitalist system that had created the boom. So, the desire to fight communism increased.

INTERPRETATION ANALYSIS

b An accusation could be very damaging – could be blacklisted – people were forced out of their jobs because of the 'disgrace' associated with their investigation. People would find it hard to find another job in order to support their family.

c Grant refused to testify against her husband at the HUAC hearings and was 'blacklisted' from most acting jobs for the next ten years. It also contributed to her divorce.

d Grant seems to think negatively about this era. This is because McCarthyism had a very negative impact on her career.

Chapter 8 Page 51
DESCRIBE

a A campaign from 1940s to late 1960s to achieve civil rights for African-Americans equal to those of white Americans.

b Your chart might include:
- President's Committee on Civil Rights: 1946. *Description:* Presidential committee that recommended 'elimination of segregation, based on race, colour, creed or national origin, from American life'. *Impact:* Government action on civil rights.

- 'Brown v Board of Education of Topeka': 1954. *Description:* Father of a black girl (Linda Brown) took local education authority to court, hoping it would end school segregation. He lost, but on appeal the Supreme Court ruled that every education board must end segregation. *Impact:* Many cities began to 'de-segregate' their schools, but segregation remained common in Southern schools.
- Montgomery Bus Boycott: 1955. *Description:* Rosa Parks, an African-American woman, refused to move from the 'whites only' section of a public bus. She was arrested. Local black community leaders called a boycott of all city buses, led by Martin Luther King, which lasted many months. Finally, the Supreme Court ruled that segregated buses, like schools, were illegal. *Impact:* Important victory for the Civil Rights Movement. Made MLK famous.
- The Little Rock case: 1957. *Description:* African-American pupils tried to attend Central High School in Little Rock, Arkansas, but were prevented. The African-Americans of Little Rock took the governor to court – and won. *Impact:* Black pupils now had the right to go to the school. But by 1962, there were still no black children attending white schools in Alabama, South Carolina or Mississippi.

c Answers might include: details from Truman's President's Committee, 'Brown v Board of Education of Topeka', the Little Rock case or the Montgomery Bus Boycott.

Page 53
IN WHAT WAYS

a Spider diagram might include:
- When: Late 1940s–1960s.
- Key individuals/groups in peaceful protest: MLK, Freedom Riders, people taking part in sit-ins, civil rights marchers etc.
- Key individuals/groups in militant protest: Malcolm X, Nation of Islam, Black Panthers.
- Key events: Sit-ins, freedom rides and marches – Alabama, Selma.
- Reforms: Civil Rights Acts of 1957, 1964 and 1968.
- Impact: Greater equality in housing, education, voting etc.

b Your answers should focus on what it was like before the movement – Jim Crow Laws and segregation – and then include a brief explanation of how a variety of both laws and popular movements tried to ensure and force greater equality in housing, education, voting, freedom to marry interracially, etc.

Chapter 9 Page 55

IN WHAT WAYS

a • New Frontier: series of domestic programmes introduced by JFK to tackle poverty, inequality, poor education and unemployment.
   • Great Society: series of domestic reforms introduced by LBJ to make America a better, fairer place.

b Write your own revision cards.

c You should write about the successes of LBJ's Great Society in relation to the economy (Job Corps helped high school leavers get jobs, minimum wage increased, etc.), healthcare and poverty (Housing Act funded low-income housing, Model Cities Act cleared up inner-city slums etc.) and education ('Operation Headstart' gave money to poor schools, VISTA programme set up as a domestic version of the Peace Corps etc.). You could also write summative sentences – the percentage of African-Americans living in desperate poverty dropped, for example. You should mention some negatives as examples of how the promise was not fulfilled – by 1968, unemployment was rising, widespread rioting in poorer areas of some cities.

Page 57

DESCRIBE

a • NOW: demanded complete equal rights for women in US law – high profile, many members, wrote to politicians, organised large demonstrations and took to court companies that failed to pay women the same wages as men.
   • Equal Rights Amendment: sought to change the law so that 'Equality of rights under the law shall not be denied by the United States or by any State on account of sex.' However, it was defeated, so had limited impact, but stirred debate.
   • 'Stop ERA': set up to fight the Equal Rights Amendment. The leader (Phyllis Schlafly) argued that ERA would lead to women in combat, more abortions, unisex bathrooms and homosexual marriages. Stop ERA had a negative impact on women's rights as it defeated ERA.
   • 'Roe v Wade' case: high impact, raised profile of the abortion issue and created national debate. The ruling finally meant women could make their own decision on abortion.

b You should pick and briefly write about two ways in which the actions of people attempted to improve women's rights – for example, Betty Friedan, NOW or 'Roe v Wade'.

INTERPRETATION ANALYSIS

b 1 **A** is very positive about the movement; it says it had great impact, was revolutionary, and changed everything for women – socially, economically, politically. **B** argues that the movement didn't have this impact, and that gender equality has not yet been achieved.

2 Different people have different views. The author of **A** was a teenager in the 1970s, so is more likely to have been at the radical end of the movement. She is speaking on a film that may be skewed towards showing the greater impact. The author of **B** was older, perhaps better educated, so takes a more balanced view.

3 Both interpretations are convincing, as both recognise achievements of the feminist movement. As **A** suggests, the women's liberation movement achieved an Equal Pay Act in 1963 and contributed to a Civil Rights Act in 1964. In 1973 feminist movements campaigned for the legal right to abortion. All these achievements happened through the law-making and legal system. Although the law can change, attitudes are harder to influence. Some women campaigned against equal rights such as the 'Stop ERA' campaign in 1972. As **B** says, although women gained legal rights, in reality many remained economically second-class. In 1963 only 4% of lawyers, and 7% of doctors were women and women earned 60% less than men. That did not change much.

B

blacklist a list of people or groups regarded as unacceptable and often treated badly or punished

buying on the margin a method of buying shares where an investor pays just 10 per cent of the share price, then pays the remaining amount with the profits they make when the shares are sold

C

Civil Rights Movement the campaign for equal opportunity and access to employment, housing and education, as well as the right to vote and the right to be free of racial discrimination

constitution the system of laws and basic principles that a country is governed by

consumer goods goods that people buy

consumerism the concept that the ever-expanding consumption of goods benefits the economy

containment an American policy that tried to stop the spread of communism

D

Democratic Party one of the two main political parties in US politics; often seen as more liberal

F

feminist movement organisations that work for improved women's rights; sometimes called the 'women's movement'

flapper usually a rich young woman who shocked older Americans with her independent behaviour

G

Great Depression the very serious economic crisis that hit America after the Wall Street Crash in 1929 and lasted for most of the 1930s; too many goods were produced, not enough people bought them and millions lost their jobs

Great Society President Lyndon Johnson's programme of reforms that aimed to make America a better, fairer society

H

hire purchase plan a way of purchasing goods by paying in small instalments over a long period

HUAC (House of Representatives Un-American Activities Committee) an organisation set up to search for communists working for the government, in workplaces, the media and in the Hollywood movie industry

I

isolationism the idea that America should not play an important role in European concerns but concentrate instead on what is happening domestically

J

jazz a popular musical style associated with the 1920s

L

laissez-faire a French phrase meaning 'leave alone'; a policy that limited the government's role in people's lives or in the running of businesses

Lend Lease March 1941 policy which saw America 'lend' (rather than sell) weapons to Britain

lynch to kill without a trial, usually by hanging

M

McCarthyism the campaign against alleged communists named after Senator Joseph McCarthy, a US politician who accused hundreds of people of being communists in the 1950s

O

organised crime groups of people, often called gangsters, who work together to break the law; they often run their criminal activities like a business

P

persecution the mistreatment of an individual or group by another

Prohibition the ban on alcohol in America from 1920 to 1933

R

radical extreme ideas that advocate complete political or social change

Republican Party one of the two main political parties in US politics; often seen as more conservative

reservation an area of land set aside for use by American Indians

S

segregate to keep separate

sharecropper a farmer who rented a small area of land from a landowner; they had to give a share of their crop to this landlord

stock market a place where investors buy and sell shares; in America, the stock market is situated on Wall Street, New York

superpower one of the countries in the world that has very great military or economic power and a lot of influence, for example America